SO YOU WANT
TO BE A DANCER

SO YOU WANT TO BE A DANCER

Practical Advice and True Stories from a Working Professional

MATTHEW SHAFFER

TAYLOR TRADE PUBLISHING
Lanham • Boulder • New York • London

Published by Taylor Trade Publishing
An imprint of The Rowman & Littlefield Publishing Group, Inc.
4501 Forbes Boulevard, Suite 200, Lanham, Maryland 20706
www.rowman.com

Unit A, Whitacre Mews, 26-34 Stannary Street, London SE11 4AB

Distributed by NATIONAL BOOK NETWORK

British Library Cataloguing in Publication Information Available

Library of Congress Cataloging-in-Publication Data Available
ISBN 978-1-63076-026-7 (cloth : alk. paper) —
ISBN 978-1-63076-027-4 (electronic)

∞ ™ The paper used in this publication meets the minimum requirements of
American National Standard for Information Sciences—Permanence of Paper
for Printed Library Materials, ANSI/NISO Z39.48-1992.

Printed in the United States of America

My journey as a dancer has manifested into a wonderful career thanks to the unending love and support of my family and friends who continue to inspire me to do my best, trust my instincts, and follow my heart.

I dedicate this book to Grandma and Grandpa Shaffer, who reminded me to never give up; to Grandma and Grandpa Smith, for never missing a performance; to my mom, who remains my number one fan; to my dad, who drove me forty-five miles every day to attend a performing-arts high school; to my sister, who taught me to be a fighter; and to Jeff Payton, who challenges me to be a better person and artist every single day.

Contents

Special Thanks

I offer my deepest gratitude and special thanks to each of these experts for collaborating with me to encourage you:

Zetta Alderman, Lacy Baxter, Darlene Bejnar, Rita Maye Bland, Debby Boone, Ellen Buckley, Craig Burns, Pam Chancey, Steve Chetelat, Kacy Combs, Joseph Corella, Sandra Coyte, Grover Dale, Marguerite Derricks, John Dietrich, Tyce Diorio, Brian Dreyfuss, Melissa Fagan, Alex Monti Fox, Aisha Francis, Troy Garza, Gus Giordano, Nan Giordano, Devert Hickman, Bernadette Hill, Lorie Faith Holtey, Gigi Hunter, Jim Keith, Beckie King, Brooke Kivowitz, Lisa Lindholm, Terry Lindholm, Richard Lissemore, Nicholas Pere MacLeod, Anthony Marciona, Shannon Mather, Michael McBride, Melissa McComas, Julie McDonald, Maggie Miguel, Mike Canale Photography, Autumn Miller, Krista Miller, Megan Mullally, Torri Oats, Nancy O'Meara, Ralph Opacic, Kristy Pace, Noelle Pate Packett, Chris Paltin, Gary Pate, Travis Payne, Christine Paynton, Jeff Payton, Bevin Allen Pike, Rick Rinehart, Samuel Lee Roberts,

Joan Rosenfels, Melissa Sandvig, Karie Simpson, Tracie Stanfield, Rick Sullivant, Nadine Tayir-Lewis, Stacey Tookey, Yvette Tucker, Grace Wakefield, Stacy Walker, Susan Quinn Williams, Lakey Wolff, and Michelle Zeitlin, and a very special thanks to Julia Cameron and *The Artist's Way* for encouraging me to write!

Overture

I F YOU happen to be the proud parent of a child who dances, the question-filled parent of a child who wants to become a dancer, or a dancer ready to embark on a professional career, congratulations on the purchase of this book. The stories I share will provide a backstage tour of the life of a dancer. From my first class I knew what I wanted to do with my future. As much as I was grateful to my loving and supportive parents, sometimes as a performer you have to take matters into your own hands.

I was only thirteen years old. In addition to the insults and name-calling, middle school had brought about a revelation and a serious, life-changing moment. When most young boys were playing He-Man, swapping baseball cards, and perfecting their BMX wheelies, "by the power of Grayskull" I was going to conquer the entertainment business. I swapped out my Boy Scout uniform and Swiss Army knife for jazz shoes and a glossy headshot.

Inspired by *Fame*—and the gossip around the water fountain among the older teenage dancers at an audition for the sixty-fourth Academy Awards with legendary choreographer Debbie Allen (who really is going to live forever)—I decided that I *needed* to attend the Orange County High School of the Arts. (Every parent reading this surely knows the difference between "need" and "*need*.") A school dedicated to the training and development of dance, theater, and the art of accepting your creative individuality? Yes, please!

Unbeknownst to my parents, I decided to do some #Pre-Internet research. I secured an application from my vice principal and requested glowing recommendations from my dance and drama teachers. I filled out this application in my own handwriting and waited for a response.

My parents discovered that I had enrolled myself at OCHSA without telling them when they received an appointment for my

> **#DanceNote**
>
> Every young dancer wants to win a platinum trophy; very few are willing to accept gold as part of the growth process.

entrance audition addressed directly to them. Needless to say, they weren't pleased that I had reached out without their permission, but they recognized my determination and resourcefulness and allowed me to audition anyway. To my delight, I was accepted into the Commercial Dance Department. Somehow I convinced my dad to commit to driving me to and from

Say *cheese*! My first headshot in LA

school every day! Trust me, that hour-long car ride was invaluable bonding time. My journey at OCHSA provided the foundation for the rest of my career.

As you probably realize, there isn't "one" singular way to "make it" in this industry. Yet convincing a headstrong artist (regardless of age) to do something other than follow their passion is like convincing a movie critic that Madonna* can act. People who want to succeed always find a way! Hopefully this book offers some practical wisdom and sparks a laugh or two along the way.

> **#DanceNote**
>
> The difference between a soloist and an ensemble dancer is approximately ten more hours of training a week.
> #Ballet

Important Note

I am an expert at absolutely everything. Just ask me. However, my parents, through their recently hired lawyer, insist I remind you that I am not. The events I write of and advice I share in this book are based on my career in the entertainment industry. Though some events and names have been reinterpreted (as artists often do), the stories are real. I offer my hard-earned advice as inspiration but make no guarantees about your future. I'm still on a path to discovering mine!

---

* P.S. I L-O-V-E #Madonna.

Curtain Up!

AROUND THE time that I was taking my first steps as a toddler, I can remember a moment when I was sitting in front of a gigantic, self-standing box made out of dark brown wood with giant plastic dials.* Just on the other side of the glass, vibrant people mesmerized me as they sang and danced. I sat in front of the television set all day trying to figure out how to get in that box and be a part of the magic I was watching.

I was hooked. From then on, everything I did became a theatrical event. I used the coffee table in our living room as a stage and performed my very own cabaret. Bath time turned into "Singing in the Tub." Household chores turned into a scene from *Annie*. It didn't matter if I had an audience or not. Grocery shopping was the best because I had those big aisles with the linoleum floors, ideal for my rubber-soled shoes that would squeak like tap shoes as I sang and danced along the

---

* For those of you born in the twenty-first century, Google *old-fashioned television set*.

Early in my dance career (please note the strong parallel second position but weak #JazzHands!)

canned-food section. It was like one giant set, and all the other shoppers were the extras in my big show. I still fight the urge to do chassé switch leaps every time I'm in a grocery store.

It was abundantly clear that my parents had no hope of my becoming a doctor, lawyer, civil engineer, or anything other than a performer when I grew up. Thankfully they encouraged me to follow my passion, and don't think I didn't take advantage of that. I exploited every family reunion, wedding, and company picnic with my off-off-off-Broadway shows. Captive audiences became the perfect showtime.

I was confident that I had my supportive parents convinced of my creative genius. However, it wasn't until two larger-than-life heroes entered my world that it occurred to me that I could dream bigger.

The first time I saw *Thriller* I was blown away. Michael Jackson's showmanship and talent was totally #Rad, as we'd say in the 1980s. I was obsessed with studying Michael's every move and mannerisms. I learned the choreography to every video so that I would be ready to step in as soon as I received the call from the Gloved One. (Because that fantasy plays out in your head when you're nine years old.) My dreams really took flight soon after watching the movie *Dirty Dancing*.

> **#DanceNote**
>
> Pick one thing that you learned by watching a peer perform and incorporate it into your daily dance practice.

I was nine years old when I snuck into the living room past my bedtime to watch an R-rated movie with *dance* in the title.

Patrick Swayze made working as a dance teacher at a country club look like the most glamorous job ever. (The adrenaline from secretly watching the movie and excitement from being up past my bedtime may have heightened the cool factor.) Regardless, Patrick demonstrated his talent as a well-trained dancer, singer, and actor. Plus, he got the girl in the end. Sign me up. I wanted to be just like him.

VHS tapes* were still coveted phenomena at the time, and my parents loved to collect them, so naturally they bought *Dirty Dancing*. Every day for two months I would play the tape before

---

* Kids, a *VHS*—or *video home system*—player is an oversized electronic instrument used to watch movies at home, often bulky, and seriously out of date. I'd compare it to a DVD player, but you probably don't know what that is either. It's like watching Apple TV, only you had to buy the movies at a video store. Okay, never mind.

they came home from work. Like a Russian ballet mistress, I'd force my sister to rehearse the dance steps just like we saw in the movie.

Around the same time, my parents were invited to a lavish wedding at the Ambassador Hotel in Los Angeles, and children were welcome. I felt like a movie star from the moment I walked into that hotel ballroom. The sound of the live band filled that enormous room with magnificent energy. As the night progressed I could hardly contain myself from exploding on the dance floor. Once I'd consumed enough cake to ensure a sugary high, I found the courage to approach the bandleader. Without my parents knowing, I requested "The Time of My Life," the finale song from *Dirty Dancing*.

> **#DanceNote**
>
> The entertainment industry is small and connected. Build relationships, not rivalries.

As the first chord vibrated through the crowd, I had my sister up out of her chair and on the floor. I felt like a bigger celebrity than Justin Bieber, dancing our choreographed routine to the live music in that grand ballroom. (I'm positive our performance would have rivaled any seen on the Grammys.) By the end of the song, my sister and I were the only two people left standing in the middle of the parquet floor. It was silent for a minute, and then a roar of applause and laughter filled the room. My parents approached us in a state of shock and delight. Obviously they had questions that would be answered later in the evening at home, but for the time being, I could see the pride on their faces.

As fate would have it, a children's entertainment agent happened to be among the guests at the wedding—and the rest (as they say) is history.

There are a million different ways that people get started in this business. Some of us have supportive families, great opportunities, and pure luck; others do not. I was fortunate to have luck on my side getting started. However, the journey has taken me down many rough roads. I worked very hard to pave my own way in this industry, and I did so without much knowledge of how the business side worked. There were no books on how to succeed as a dancer or which direction I should take to realize my dreams.

Though I'm now able to look back with appreciation on that part of my journey, my goal with this book is to present some answers to the questions I had when I was getting started on my own. I hope that the stories I share and the advice I offer will add inspiration, encouragement, and practical answers as you embark on your journey as an artist. No matter what, the best advice I can offer is to never give up!

Right to the Pointe

#TalentCompetitions

The sequins, glue gun, and hair extensions are packed, and you are set for another weekend of showstopping competition. Like many of you, I also started out as a competition dancer. Now, thanks to that training (and the career that I have worked so hard on), I'm fortunate enough to experience competitions from the other side of the judges' table. I love the opportunities that dance competitions provide.

Aside from the obvious experience you gain as a performer, competitions offer a unique perspective into what your life will be like as a professional. The competition dancer learns how to handle the pressure of remembering a massive amount of choreography, perfecting a quick change, and improvising when you forget choreography. You make friends and develop networking skills that will help you as a professional in the industry. People with negative things to say about dance competitions fail to recognize the amount of dedication, hard work,

The dance moms are all smiles when an industry insider is near!

and creativity involved. Just like any other athlete, a competitive dancer will endure tough love. In this industry you'd better get used to that early.

At every competition I judge, I'm inspired by the artistry and remarkable advancements that dancers make at such a young age. The future of dance relies on the fearlessness of the up-and-coming innovators who often emerge from the competition world. The challenge is learning how to transition into a professional career from that world.

> **#DanceNote**
>
> Working on tricks will help you win competitions. Working on technique will help you become a working dancer!

#TechnicallySpeaking

Young dancers often spend much of their time perfecting competition choreography and building on technique, which of course serves its purpose. You have to remember that audiences pay big money to be entertained. The most important job you have as a dancer is to master the art of performing. You are a storyteller, and technique is just the beginning. It is essential that you convey the emotional journey that corresponds with the choreographer's piece.

> **#DanceNote**
>
> Overusing pirouette combinations in your choreography is like using the same word over and over and over and over and over again in a sentence. Eventually it becomes ineffective and uncreative.

Everyone hates listening when old people tell them what to do, so just pretend I'm the most popular kid in your school right now. *Okay, so, like, it would be sooo amazing if you understood how important it is to, like, be a well-rounded dancer. For reals. You totally, like, have to do your job as a dancer and, like, expand on your training as an actor and singer. Seriously, like, the more polished and amazing you can be as a performer, like, the more you will for sure work as a dancer!*

It is easy to watch other dancers in class or on stage and critique their technical ability. But how often do you enjoy another dancer from the audience's point of view? The average audience member has no idea what flawless technique looks like. I promise they will always prefer watching a captivating performer over a perfect dancer. For example, did you watch *Black Swan* and think, "OMG, Natalie Portman is such a brilliant dancer"? *No.* Still, I bet you got caught up in the emotion she conveyed as an actor.

Passion and natural charisma have a lot to do with that, but so does hard work. It is not enough to learn a phrase of choreography. You have to explore the layers in the movement and connect with them emotionally. A piece of choreography has a storyline, just like your favorite movie, with an arc and a journey that the audience goes on while watching the performance. As a dancer, you have to analyze the choreography exactly like an actor would study a script. Find the beats in the story. Understand the movement and how it relates to the "character" you play while performing the choreography. Discovering as a dancer how to properly connect with the dance will make you stand out above the corp.

> **#DanceNote**
>
> Dancers must maintain their confidence while releasing their egos. Finding that balance takes more than a strong center and high relevé. It requires growing from your failures.

In every major city there are acting and vocal classes geared toward dancers. Find a class where you feel safe and supported. I know how hard it is for dancers to use their voices. Just like Lilly in *Pitch Perfect*, it scares us to express ourselves with our voices because we have spent our entire lives "talking" with our bodies. Nevertheless, if you want your name to #Trend on Twitter, you have to pivot step away from your comfort zone and go for it. Trust me, any trained dancer can learn how to act and sing. You may not be the next Kelly Clarkson, but at least you'll gain confidence in yourself as an artist. The more comfortable you feel using your real voice, the easier it will be to connect with and relate to the choreography you perform.

#Bullying

So many people I know have felt picked on at some point in their lives. Despite the schoolyard bullying and inevitable clichés, I was ready to be the next overachieving Billy Elliot. Waiting for the end of the school day was as challenging as fighting the urge to lip-synch to any Katy Perry song. I had heard the endless discretionary tales of a dancer's life and how hard it is to make it. Naturally, I ignored the warnings like I would ignore a plateful of disgusting mushrooms. (I *hate* mushrooms, but if you happen to love them, please insert the food of your choice that offers the same level of revulsion!)

I was nine years old the first time I entered a dance studio. The intoxicating smell of ambition, sweat, and leather Capezio jazz oxfords permeated the hardwood floors. (It was the first time in my life that a scent other than food got me excited!) I stood on the threshold between the carpeted waiting room and the dance floor filled with stunning dancers. Two at a time, they soared through the air with relentless passion.

I looked back at my mom and dad and uttered the words that my father had been dying to hear from his only son for soccer, baseball, football, or any other sport ending in -*ball*. "Sign me up!" Without hesitation, my parents enrolled me in Beginning Teen Jazz, and my journey began.

During the first three years of dance, most of my grade school friends had no idea that I spent every Thursday night perfecting my #JazzHands with a room full of girls.

By the time I reached middle school, I could no longer hide my enthusiasm. It was not a hobby; I was not "collecting" dance. It was much more significant to me than a sport. I watched my friends play sports, and most of them hated it. I *loved* to dance.

I was fully committed to becoming a professional dancer, and I wasn't concerned with anyone else's judgment. Or so I thought.

Everyone who survived junior high knows how devastatingly cruel tweenagers can be. Nowadays we use the term #Bullying. When I was growing up, it was just a part of my everyday life. At first, the negative comments and painful attacks on my character just stung. I'd seen *Can't Buy Me Love,** so I was prepared for the usual teenage taunting. However, as I continued to pursue dance, the "jokes" turned into torment.

Let me set the stage: I was freakishly short for my age and very round. I wore dress pants from the Macy's "husky" department with vintage button-down dress shirts from my grandpa's closet. To make matters worse, I had developed a serious case of acne from all of the stress. (Imagine a fabulously styled Mr. Potato Head with a pepperoni pizza face.) So yeah, that was fun.

---

* Substitute *Sixteen Candles, Clueless, 10 Things I Hate about You, Mean Girls*, or any other decade-appropriate teen-angst movie.

My sister and me backstage after a performance #Neon'90s

Several kids spent every lunch period harassing me to the point where I could no longer eat in the cafeteria. Others would follow me between classes shouting, "Butterball," "Fatty," "Gayboy," and other hateful slurs.

I ignored the situation until rumors wound their way through the nasty schoolyard grapevine and into my little sister's ears. She was so devastated by the evil words that I actually considered quitting dance.

I begged her not to tell my parents, because I was embarrassed that I was being made fun of. I spent every night crying myself to sleep, praying that the kids would stop so that I could keep doing what I loved.

The bullying continued until one day, in seventh grade, the anger and rage boiling inside motivated me to stand up and roar back. (Imagine a clip from *When Animals Attack!* on the Discovery Channel.) I was the lone hyena attacking the lions to shreds. Needless to say, from then on kids avoided me like an A-list actress avoids carbs.

Once I got to high school, I discovered that the kids who harassed me saw something in me that terrified them. They realized I was a confident person working toward a remarkable goal. I wasn't afraid to stand out or be different, and they couldn't control that.

Thankfully, around the same time I found a group of friends who valued my individuality and determination. I had also refined my skills as a smart-mouthed class comedian who could retaliate with a joke so ferocious it would knock the bully off his feet and have everyone laughing.*

Kids can be downright hateful. Still, if it weren't for my past, I wouldn't be writing this book and sharing my experiences with you. Don't let anyone define who you are or what you are capable of. Follow your passion, and trust in your path. You control your future.

---

* Sometimes you have to fight fire with fire.

#WeightThere'sMore

I'm not a nutritionist or celebrity trainer like Tracy Anderson, and this is not *The Biggest Loser: Book Edition*. However, as dancers, we definitely need to have a conversation about health and our bodies, especially because we spend more time in front of the mirror than Snow White's wicked stepmother!

At thirteen years old, I decided to skip a meal for the first time. I was dancing all day long and couldn't figure out why I was gaining weight. It never occurred to me that puberty had hit and that my body was undergoing big changes. Unfortunately, I developed an eating disorder, a problem that only got worse with people's positive praise of my "new" physique. As the problem persisted, I experienced exhaustion and fatigue, and my dancing started to suffer. At one point, I couldn't even make it through an entire class without getting dizzy or losing focus. Simply put, I was not eating enough food to maintain the amount of hours I was dancing, and the food I *was* eating offered no nutritional substance. Thankfully, at this point my parents and dance teachers noticed, and together we sought a doctor's support to implement

#DanceNote

Fact: Favoring your "good side" will not help you transition as a professional dancer. Every pirouette, turn combo, and tilt you do on the right *should* be practiced on the left, too!

healthier eating habits and achieve nutritional goals in line with my professional aspirations.

Throughout my teenage years my weight fluctuated, but it was generally because I was getting ready to go through a major growth spurt. I focused on staying healthy and positive about my body at every stage. By the time I was eighteen, I thought I was back on track and more confident about my body, until I attended an audition for a scholarship to Giordano Dance Chicago. During the grueling five-hour audition, the male dancers were asked to take off their shirts. I *hated* dancing shirtless. Even though I was eighteen years old, I was really underdeveloped. Thanks to the lack of good eating habits when I had been younger, my limbs looked more like toothpicks than timber, and I had a "soft-pack" where there should have been a six-pack. Let's just say I was no Zac Efron! I was so self-conscious and embarrassed that I totally forgot most of the choreography and was positive I was not going to receive a scholarship.

Shockingly, three weeks later, my scholarship notice arrived in the mail, and I was off to Chicago to begin my training with Giordano Dance Chicago. Apparently they'd seen past my self-inflicted (and ridiculous)

> **#DanceNote**
>
> The only place you'll ever find "technique" after "performance" is in the dictionary. And remember, "ballet" comes before both!

body insecurities and realized my potential as a talented dancer. While I was in the scholarship program,
I worked with a nutritionist and began to understand
how important it is to eat well-balanced meals regularly. I started an intense fitness program, incorporating
weight lifting and cardio. For the first time in my life,
I began to feel confident and proud of my hard work
and got to enjoy food, too!

The moral of the story is to take care of yourself, eat well, and be confident in who you are during every stage of your development. The entertainment industry sets unrealistic demands on society, and we can easily fall victim to the criticism of our peers. The images you see in magazines have been altered and send negative messages to dancers and nondancers alike. I am not a doctor, a psychologist, or even your dance teacher, and I want to be perfectly clear that I am not telling you how to eat or workout. There will be plenty of people throughout your career who will tell you all the things that are "wrong" with you, to "Fix this," "Change that," "Do this," "Do that!"

The practical advice I'm offering is to love and take care of yourself throughout your career, to be proud of your talent, and to seek help from professionals to make healthy life choices. Take advantage of the time you have as young dancer to explore as many styles as possible. Rather than focusing on nailing fifteen pirouettes to the right, make sure you can do three pirouettes to the left, too! Most importantly, work on achieving a greater connection to the emotion of your performance. You might not always win first overall, but in order to succeed as a professional you have to accept that this industry (unlike dance competitions) doesn't hand out first-place trophies to everyone who auditions.

Degree or Not Degree

T HE NUMBER one question young dancers ask me is, "Should I go to college?" My short response is, "*You must answer this question for yourself.*" #Seriously. You decide what clothes you want to wear, pictures you post to the world, friends you hang out with, and music you listen to, so why wouldn't you take an active role in deciding your future?

As you approach the end of your high school journey, you (and your parents, mentor, or guidance counselor) may question your next step. Should you go to college or start auditioning? A college degree often unlocks the door to a better life with an extraordinary career, salary, and benefits. In many instances, if you don't hold a degree, you won't get the job.

The reality is, even with a degree, you will most likely start your dance career the same way everyone else does: packed into a room full of dancers who look just like you, learning a challenging and somewhat awkward combination. Even after you are discovered as the next Julianne Hough, odds are you will still have to audition for gigs alongside dancers of all different levels. Some will be just starting out, and many will have résumés a mile long. In that moment, your ability to nail the choreography and look the part—not a college degree—will determine whether or not you book the job. That's right! The glamorous life of a dancer involves #Auditioning at every stage of your career.

Wait! Before you melt down like a reality TV star who just found out her show has been *cancelled* and scream at your parents for forcing you to go to school, ask yourself, "If I don't need a degree to work as a dancer, why should I go to college?"

> **#DanceNote**
>
> #Twerking might get you a job on MTV, but #Working on your technique will secure a strong future as a professional dancer!

Excellent question. I'm delighted you asked!

The leap from high school into *The Real World* is not as easy as MTV makes it look. Balancing a checkbook is not like balancing on relevé. Unless you are a trust-fund socialite like Paris Hilton, life on your own requires working a job to pay for things like food and a place to sleep. Going to college can often ease the transition and help introduce you to life without your mom and dad. In college you will be able to explore your independence and still enjoy the comfort of dorm life.

Attending a university or conservatory provides an ideal way to discover a new city and establish yourself as a dancer in that market. You might find opportunities to perform at local theme parks and theaters, enabling you to build your professional résumé and make money while pursuing a higher education.

If you thought knowing the right people only mattered on *Pretty Little Liars*, guess again! One of the prime arguments for attending a top-notch university is the connections you will make. Introductions are important in every field, and the entertainment industry is no exception. Even if you are the most phenomenal dancer in the room, as soon as you get cut from your first audition you will discover that it helps to know the choreographer or director.

I suspect the last thing you want to do is more homework,* but it pays to do some research before choosing a college or conservatory. Check out the alumni success rates. Where are they after they graduate? Will they be in a position to help you later on in your career? Whether starting off in college or skipping straight to Broadway, you want to secure lasting relationships with talented people eager to succeed. At the risk of sounding like a host plugging zit cream on an infomercial, I want to repeat: you have to establish a network of friends and colleagues that you will collaborate with throughout your career.

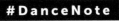

#DanceNote

Be your own judge! Record yourself while you do a ballet barre to see what you can improve on.

---

* I've supplied a #CheatSheet for you in the Encore, filled with a comprehensive list of universities with exceptional dance programs and *more* advice. You're welcome!

#PlanB

I have never been a fan of the what-if or just-in-case scenarios, primarily because I'm a firm believer in working hard and accomplishing my goals. If you are serious about becoming a professional dancer, you must accept that there is absolutely *no* guarantee that you will make it, whether you have a degree or not. I will say I am an advocate of continued education. The learning process should never stop, even after school. Attending college should be a choice you make because you want to prepare for your future, meet new friends, and establish yourself as an adult. If you are going to party and skip classes for shopping sprees in the city, then you are wasting a lot of money and valuable training. College gives you a platform from which to leap, *not* a safety net in which to land.

> **#DanceNote**
>
> Technique includes learning terminology. Grab a dance dictionary, and learn the proper names and spelling of the elements you perform.

#What'sYourMajor?

Most dancers automatically assume that they should major in dance. Depending on the university or conservatory you attend, the dance program may very well require a serious commitment. But here's the deal: unless you want to earn a master's degree and become a professor or an artistic director of a company, that degree isn't necessarily adding value to your career as an actual dancer.

Consider double majoring in business, English, history, or communications. If you are going to invest in your future, you might as well earn a degree that you will use every day in the industry. A deeper understanding of the world in which we live only adds to your creative catalogue and provides more insight

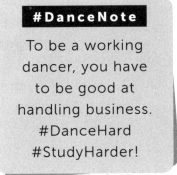

#DanceNote

To be a working dancer, you have to be good at handling business. #DanceHard #StudyHarder!

into what you'll bring to the table as a performer. As soon as you leave college and begin your career in entertainment, you'll discover why it's called show *business*.

#NoMoreSchool

Like Lea Michele, Zac Efron, Taylor Swift, and Tyra Banks, some of you may choose to not attend college. Obviously, you are in good company, but remember that no matter how remarkable *you* know you are, there is no assurance you'll become a star.

The wonderful aspect of a career in entertainment is that you can perform almost anywhere in the world, at any age. Wherever there is an audience looking to escape reality, there's a job opportunity for you. If you want to skip the BFA* program to perform in the concert-dance world, pay close attention to chapter 4. Or perhaps you will decide to begin your career performing on a cruise ship. Cruises offer a rewarding, safe way to travel the world, make money, and gain experience. Theme parks

---

* A *BFA*—or *bachelor of fine arts*—is an even more-focused and -prestigious course of study. This will mean more time working on your craft and less time on the quad.

offer résumé-building experience, too! I know several dancers who put themselves through college by working six-month contracts on cruise ships between each year of school. They banked money, added credits to their résumés, and made mom and dad proud parents. I'm just giving you options, people. NEWS FLASH: There's more information on cruise ships and theme parks in the Encore.

I think we all agree that reading this chapter has been almost as enjoyable as taking a college-entrance exam. We made it, though, and now you have a more-enlightened view of your options. Inevitably, the decision is up to you. I urge you to take the leading part in your story. Be brave! Success as a performer requires an unimaginable leap of faith. I've learned that you have plenty of time to work in this business. As you get older, you may face more challenges in terms of ability; however, you are never too old to work. Just ask Chita Rivera!* True, there are some fields of dance where time is of the essence. If you want to perform in a ballet or concert-dance company, it might make more sense to jump right into their training programs. If you decide to choose a path in musical theater, college is an ideal place to develop your craft and build strong bonds. Take a note from your dance training: wherever you focus your spot is where you will finish your turn!

> **#DanceNote**
>
> If your foot is sickled in your preparation, it will most likely be sickle in your jump or pirouette, too!

---

* If you don't instantly recognize that name, please stop right here and Google her. I'll wait.

The "Blue Collar" Concert Dancer

I F YOU dream of getting paid to take classes, rehearse all day, and perform the innovative work of world-class choreographers in beautiful theaters around the globe, then you are going to #Love life as a concert dancer. But don't punk yourself into believing that your life will be filled with Louis Vuitton luggage and Prada shoes. You'll be grateful when you can afford to treat yourself to a Starbucks triple espresso after a six-hour rehearsal on the way to teaching eight-year-olds #JazzHands in order to pay your roommate the rent on which you are three days overdue!

By choosing the life of a concert dancer, you commit yourself to a lifelong journey of fulfilling artistry and personal passion. The exhilaration of doing what you love all day, every day, is the ultimate payoff. I compare a concert dancer to a blue-collar worker, because, like most trade workers, dancers follow a clear-cut path. If you do, you may find yourself performing alongside your dance heroes.

Most professional concert-dance companies have schools that filter into their programs. While on scholarship, you'll be learning the technique and style of the company. If asked to continue on after the training period ends, you will likely be appointed to an apprenticeship. As an apprentice you earn the privilege of learning the company's repertory, taking classes with principal company members, and occasionally performing with the company—all without pay. That's right, you get to spend the entire day (and most of the evening) dancing for *free*!

#DanceNote

For a professional dancer, technique isn't optional— it's job security! #Ballet

After several seasons as an apprentice, you may be promoted to a performing apprentice with pay. If you manage to survive the constant critique and freshman-like hazing similar to the verbal abuse you would see in an after-school made-for-TV special, you might enjoy the opportunity to audition to be a full-fledged company dancer.

As a concert dancer, you will get paid to tour around the world while establishing yourself as a professional. You may walk out of a stage door in Germany to a massive crowd of screaming fans begging for your autograph.

> I remember waking up on a tour bus somewhere in the middle of Germany. If it hadn't been for the pillow lines marking my face, I would have thought I was still

A studio shot of me during my time at Giordano Dance Chicago
Source: Mike Canale Photography

dreaming! After the previous night's performance, we had been stuffed into our tour bus for an eight-hour ride, arriving just in time for an early-morning technical rehearsal before another two-show day.

Here I am, nineteen years old and traveling the world, performing in theaters that are older than my first ballet teacher. (Trust me, she was *old*.) Still tired and always

With Gus Giordano after my first performance
with Giordano Dance Chicago

starving (because I have an endless appetite and am
positive I could beat a five hundred–pound ogre in a hot-
dog-eating contest), I unfold myself from the cramped
seat I am using as a bed. Once inside the new venue, I
rush to the bathroom,* and finally I am on stage to begin
our tech rehearsal. Following tech, we do a company
warm-up and trickle into the dressing room to preset our
own costumes and put on makeup. As soon as the show
begins, I feel adrenaline that I can only imagine is similar
to what Honey Boo Boo Child feels every time she enjoys
her go-go juice. European audiences love American jazz
dance. Germans especially treat us like celebrities (and

---

* Did I mention that the bus we toured Europe in for three months
didn't have a restroom?

Jump with Giordano Dance Chicago, circa 1998
Source: Mike Canale Photography

this is ten years before the paparazzi will take celebrity to
the Brangelina level.) After a ten-minute standing ovation,
a mass of fans bombards us at the stage door for pictures
and autographs. When our tour is over, we return home,
and normal life resumes: six-hour daily rehearsals, ballet
classes, lengthy gym workouts, and, finally . . . our paycheck. It is bittersweet. I am elated that I am doing what
I love. The money hardly pays my rent or fills my fridge.
Forget about buying clothes, entertainment, acting
classes, train fare, and starting that hobby of collecting
rare gems. #Sarcasm. I discover I either have to wait
tables, teach classes, or expand into other areas of the
performing arts.

So, what do you do if you adore the lack of sleep, hours of rehearsal, and endless touring and performing around the world that comes with the concert-dance lifestyle but can't pay the rent?

Most concert dancers teach dance classes at neighborhood schools, choreograph for local high school dance teams, and work random gigs as motivational dancers for parties and corporate events. Teaching offers a brilliant way to grow as a choreographer, expand your ability as a dancer, and inspire the next generation. But not all dancers want to teach, and if this is true for you, you may prefer working at a restaurant or retail store.

> **#DanceNote**
>
> Success takes work. So does a pirouette! Ballet is an excellent place to start.

Either way, it is very likely that, despite your success in the concert-dance world (wonderful reviews and covers of *Dance Magazine* aside), you will find yourself hunting for a secondary source of income. Very few concert-dance companies pay enough to sustain a lifestyle; even fewer provide health insurance or benefits.

The last thing I want to be is another hater trying to convince you to not follow your heart. Trust me, I'm on your side.* Just be sure you understand that your passion and dedication must be invincible. While you might not see a fat bank account balance, the joy of dancing across the globe, working with world-class choreographers, and performing legendary repertoire will motivate you through every obstacle that presents itself along the way.

---

* Keep in mind, I've been there and done that!

CHAPTER
5

When Dancing Explodes into Singing

I F YOU are as infatuated with dance as I am but find it harder than Gossip Girl to stop talking, then my guess is you will #Devour the world of musical theater. Like concert dance, musical theater will give you the chance to experience the thrill of a live audience while dancing—*plus* you'll get to sing and act! What with the popularity and resurgence of movie musicals and variety competition shows on TV, I'm sure you are an expert on the musical-theater universe. For those of you who have been busy perfecting the bun on your head, however, let me explain.

Similar to the point in a conversation when your BFF hits a supersonic high note describing (in elaborate detail) her date with Dreamy McSchool Jock, characters in a musical also reach a point when spoken words no longer fully express the thoughts or emotions on stage. The actors will burst into song and dance to convey the heightened excitement of the moment. Sometimes the song is subtle and small; other times it is bright and larger than life. Very often the scene unfolds into a magical dream world, inviting the audience on an inside journey of the actor's state of mind.

Some shows, like *Les Misérables*, are very dark and sad. Others, such as *Legally Blonde* or *Hairspray*, are colorful and over the top. Just like your favorite book or movie, there are musicals based on true historical events and shows that are complete works of whimsy. With such a variety of stories on Broadway during any given season, there are plenty of roles for every type of dancer to fill.

#DanceNote

Want to dance in a Broadway show? Take a voice class! You won't get a job dancing in a *chorus* if you don't sing!

In every Broadway show, there is a cast full of well-rounded ensemble performers, often called *triple threats*. Making the transition from a studio dancer to a musical-theater performer doesn't have to be as shocking as Miley Cyrus's transformation from Hannah Montana to MTV's #Twerking queen. The discipline that you have from your days in the dance studio will be a huge asset as you begin to tackle the Great White Way.

STEP ONE IN YOUR MUSICAL-THEATER METAMORPHOSIS: assess your ability as a singer and actor. It's not mandatory that you be the next star on *The Voice* in order to get a job as a dancer in a Broadway chorus. We already connect with our emotions as dancers, so the goal in becoming a well-rounded performer is to access those same emotions as we tap into our acting and singing abilities. Guess what helps you with that? If you answered, "*Lip-synching to my favorite One Direction song*," you are on the right track. In between meeting up with your scene-study partner and taking classes at Broadway Dance Center, you should begin working with a voice teacher. Just as it's important that you connect with your favorite dance classes, try taking a few lessons with various teachers until you find the person who helps you channel your inner Whitney. While working with your teacher, you will develop your voice, gain confidence, and identify with a musical style that suits your voice and personality. Are you a pop-rock punk? Or do you find standards and legit more your style?* The golden rule for dancers at a chorus call is to prepare sixteen bars each of a ballad and up-tempo song. Make sure that the songs are appropriate for the show that you are auditioning for, and work with your age range and "type."† And the only way to define your type is by enrolling in a voice class. At the risk of sounding like your mom and dad,‡ I will remind you that training is vital to a successful career. The more you are capable of, the more triple-threatening you are. Whether in a dance company or on Broadway, television, or film, the best dancers stand out because they've done their prep work. The more you grow as an artist, the more you will work. It helps if you say yes to every twist of fate that doesn't

---

* Not sure what the difference is between pop/rock and legit? You know who can fill you in? A voice coach!

† Are you a leading man or the kooky-but-hilarious girl next door? Every stereotype is a "type," and in the entertainment business, owning your type will always lead you right into a job.

‡ No offense, Mom and Dad. If you are reading this book, my guess is that you are a supercool person with exceptional taste!

compromise your moral beliefs, especially when it comes in the form of an unexpected late-night phone call!

Around the time that flip phones made their way into the hands of the average American consumer, I was joking around in a hotel room somewhere in Ohio with a group of dancers after finishing a three-day gig. In the middle of my flawless impression of Jim Carrey, my phone rang with an offer that was music to my ears.

> #DanceNote
>
> There is *no* shortcut to success—but there is always an opportunity to blaze your own path.

Weeks before, I'd had the chance to perform in a live stage show for Disney's *Hercules* at the Chicago Theatre. During the run of that show, I'd discovered that I'd really missed singing while I was working in the concert-dance company. I'd shared my desire to perform in more musicals with several of my friends in the cast, one of whom (whose brother is *still* my dance agent to this day) was searching for an immediate replacement for *The Andy Williams Show* in Branson, Missouri. She was calling me to inform me that I'd gotten the job!

At the time, I was at a crossroads in my career. Like most twenty-year-olds, I had no idea what was next for me. My only plan was to say, *"Yes!"* to every job that I was offered.

The Andy Williams Show, circa 1997

"Lighting Up the Stage" with the magnificent Debby Boone and my beautiful dance partner, Nadine Tayir-Lewis

Thankfully, while dancing in the concert-dance company, I had continued my training as a singer and actor. In between dancing all day, teaching at night, working a weekend job (to eat!), and working out (to stay fit!), I was able to squeeze in my do-re-mi's! Had I not been ready to belt out a high note, that phone call would have hit a low one.

> **#DanceNote**
>
> Your voice is a muscle; flex it every day! Try singing on your way to work or school.

I had twenty-four hours to pack my bags and get to the airport. Once I landed in Branson, I had two days to

What can I say? I look good in pink tights and a tutu. I got the job with Andy Williams because I wasn't afraid to wear a fun costume! (Trust me—I've worn worse. It's the life of a performer.)

learn the music and choreography, get fitted for costumes, and make friends with a whole new set of dancers. I remember stepping onto the stage midrehearsal and realizing I was ready to embark on a new chapter of my life. It only took me three days in the show to decide that, as soon as the run ended, I would return to Chicago, quit the concert-dance company, and move to New York!

The ideal place to switch out your ballet slippers for a pair of character shoes is New York City. The Big Apple continues to reign as the musical-theater capital of the world. The city offers a wide scope of training, creative growth, and employment. However, as YouTube has taught us, you can do virtually anything from anywhere. Don't be afraid to begin your dream anywhere there is a stage and an audience willing (or not?) to watch.

Before you rush off to DASH for your stylish opening-night wardrobe, make sure you do the preparation. You can look the part, but unless you do the work, no one will take you seriously as an actress. (Just ask Kim Kardashian.) No one expects you to be the next Anne Hathaway or Ryan Gosling overnight. The enchantment of acting class comes from learning how to create a character that marries your passion and personality with your vocal and dance ability. Flexing your acting muscle will help you grow creatively into a better dancer and open up new career opportunities as an actor.

Be careful not to mistake stage presence for acting ability. Just because you are a breathtaking dancer does not mean you are going to be an exceptional actor without training. If you have ever seen the movie *Center Stage*, you will agree that not every brilliant dancer is an equally qualified actor. I believe every dancer has the potential to be a magnificent actor, but it requires work. Similarly, it's impossible to book a job in a Broadway chorus without singing a song at your audition. Don't believe me? Then it's the perfect time for another #TrueStory.

> After packing up and moving to New York City, my first major Broadway audition was for *Cats*. And because I'd directed, choreographed, and starred in my high school's production of *Catz* (with a *z* for copyright issues), I was positive I would book the job.
>
> I showed up to the open call* with five hundred fellow feline competitors ready to meow our way to Broadway success.
>
> After signing in at the stage door, we were rounded up and placed in a line on stage. One at a time, the choreographer went down the line asking each of us to do a double pirouette and land in fourth position. Once we passed Ballet 101, he taught us several fast-paced, challenging dance combinations. Between each new combo, there was a cut. To my delight, I found myself standing among the four other guys who made it to the end of the audition. Now it was time to sing.
>
> I was freaking out, because the only thing keeping me from becoming the next Mr. Mistoffelees on Broadway was my song (a song that I had picked out in a

---

* An *open call*—often referred to as a *cattle call*—is an audition that does not require an agent or appointment. It is open to anyone who wants to audition and generally attracts hundreds of performers at a time.

Backstage at Radio City Music Hall with
Jeff Payton and Samuel Lee Roberts

panic the night before and never practiced out loud).
It was completely inappropriate for my voice and age
range. Despite the fact that I have a good voice, I was
not confident because I had stopped going to my vocal
coach. When it was my turn to sing, I sang a note so
sour, lemons were scared. From there, I forgot an entire
verse and tried to cover it up with a cough. Let's just
say, my audition (and voice) fell flat!

Afterward, the casting director reached out and informed me that they really wanted me for the part, but I would need to work on my voice. I was placed on a list and would be reconsidered the next time they were looking for a dancer. Unfortunately, *Cats* on Broadway closed six months later. Unlike my experience in Chicago, my lack of preparation for this audition lost me my first Broadway show! Me-*ouch*.

The bottom line is that you were not *born* a phenomenal dancer—you worked at it. So, do yourself a favor, and spend some time and money on your vocal and acting training too. With stellar training under your belt and the burning lights of the marquees igniting your flame, it's time to start your actual quest for *Fame*!

> **#DanceNote**
>
> In order to grow as an artist, you must push yourself past your comfort zone. Greatness is never achieved by playing it safe in class, on stage, or in life!

There are several ways you can go about getting hired for a Broadway chorus, but most of them involve waiting in long lines at the stage door. The professional-performers union, Actors' Equity Association, requires every Broadway show to hold regular chorus auditions throughout the year. Eventually, all professional musical-theater dancers must become a member of this union, but you don't have to be a member to start auditioning.* There are also plenty of trade papers and online resources to find out about auditions. Naturally, the best way to get invited

---

* We will chat more about performers' unions soon!

to audition is through your agent. But signing with an agent can be more difficult than making it into the top ten on *American Idol*!

Before you go all Nicholas Sparks dramatic on me, I'll share some good news. In chapter 7 we will cover all the juicy details of everything you need to know about agents, unions, and contracts before you audition #OMG. But, wait—there's more! In the Encore you will find a list of all the resources you will need to get started on your journey as a musical-theater performer.

Transitioning into a Broadway dancer should be a fun adventure. There will be good days and bad. There will be days when you completely blow your vocal audition, flub all of the lines on the sides* in your hands, or even forget the simplest of choreography. Yes, it's happened to all of us, and, when it does, you feel like the biggest loser. Then there will be moments when you give the best audition of your career and still get cut. No matter how many shows we have done or how talented we are, we're still people who make mistakes, sing off-key, and fall down. And the performers who make it get back up and keep on going.

---

* *Sides* are the insider's lingo for a portion of the script. Just because you're a dancer doesn't mean you're going to get out of learning lines!

Larger than Life

The alluring aroma of popcorn fills the air. Restless moviegoers all around me tweet and talk through thirty minutes of previews and clever shorts asking people to *not* tweet and talk. Finally, the lights dim, and the voices fade to a low murmur. The anticipation is *killing* me! I eagerly await the final scene in the film, when, suddenly, it happens: I see my supersized face peeking out from behind Johnny Knoxville! I will never forget the first time I saw myself in a Hollywood movie. It was a dream come true.

W ITH MOVIE STARS, fancy cars, swimming pools, and paparazzi, Los Angeles epitomizes the #GlamorousLife. Careers for dancers abound in the City of Dreams. But, fair warning, dreams can quickly turn into a nightmare worse than a blind date with Freddy Krueger. Los Angeles will only pay off if you focus and prepare.

The center of the popular-music, film, television, commercial, and print industries, Los Angeles is a playground for aspiring dancers. The trick lies in mastering the balance between work and play. Unlike New York, where the 24-7 hustle and bustle of big business serves as a constant reminder of work to be done, LA is slightly more complicated. The illusion is that nobody "works" in Los Angeles (after your second trip to Joan's on Third, you will understand where this thought comes from). The truth is that if you want to work in LA, you can never stop workin' it!

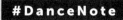

#DanceNote

Talent is something you are born with. Technique is something you develop every single day.

Between taking classes, auditioning, exercising (to keep that camera-ready physique), and working a day job to pay the bills, if you want to get on TV you will have to net*work*.

You are not the only person who moved to LA to succeed.* Whether you are at lunch, at the gym, or at the grocery store, every person you come into contact with could turn into someone who can help you realize your dreams. The people who get a leg up (hopefully turned out with a pointed foot) exude confidence and charm, excel at starting conversation, and realize that this is a business.

---

* LA is a very connected town. That diva who annoys you in dance class might someday be a choreographer who will hire you for a project. It's always better to make friends than enemies. Like Grandma Shaffer always said, "Be careful who you step on, on the way up, because they will be the ones to catch you on your way down."

Speaking of business, I know you are just dying to find out how you can twirl in the next *hot* Beyoncé video, rock the stage shaking it with Shakira, or sizzle the screen dancing with Cameron Diaz. Let's talk shop.

#MusicVideos

Thanks to iTunes, Pandora, and other online music services, the music industry has experienced a huge shift. Gone are the days of the Janet Jackson music videos with forty-five hired dancers. Think about it: Music is cheaper—great for us! But if artists are making less money, that means they're spending less money to entertain us—bad for dancers! Nevertheless, artists continue making music videos, and where there is music, there will be dancers. If you dream of dancing in a music video, then LA is the place for you. While you will enjoy seeing yourself on Vevo, YouTube, and everywhere else consumers watch music videos, don't expect to strike it rich. Unlike television and film, music videos don't fall under the same union rules, regulations, or pay scale.

A focused group of dancers, choreographers, and industry professionals continue to fight for fair working conditions and contracts for dancers in music videos. A grassroots organization founded over twenty years ago in Los Angeles, Dancers' Alliance continues to make strides in this area of dance that desperately needs boundaries.

Despite the long hours of rehearsal, the sixteen-hour shoot days, and the lack of meals or breaks, dancing in a music video can still be fun. You get to costar alongside your favorite artists, meet new dancers, and network with choreographers and directors. Music videos look great on a résumé and on your reel.*

---

* I discuss *reels* in chapter 7.

They also leave you with plenty to talk about the next time you are net*work*ing with a new agent

#ConcertTours

Every pop princess from Britney Spears to Rihanna needs to spread their music around the world if they want to sell records. The music industry spends millions of dollars conceiving and producing revolutionary live events that fill arenas around the globe. In order to keep fans purchasing tickets, these concerts have become full-scale theatrical productions, where rock roy alty reign supreme. Since most artists are #Divas, each epic event requires months of rehearsal with a team of directors, set and costume designers, sound engineers, lighting special-ists, musicians, backup sing-ers, choreographers, and, of course, dancers. That is where you step in. Unlike in music videos, dancers on tour with A-list recording artists can make great money. You get to see the world while you are young, put money in the bank (to buy a home down the road), and build your résumé while working with legends.

#DanceNote

Be inventive and creative. Get a group of friends together, and explore choreographing a hip-hop dance to classical ballet music!

#Television

Television is as important to most Americans as ex-boyfriends are to Taylor Swift's songwriting. Whether you watch TV pro-gramming on your laptop, smartphone, or tablet or consume

Kickin' It on set #Selfie!

it the good ol' fashioned way, the constantly evolving medium offers hundreds of channels featuring content that satisfies every genre. To a dancer, that translates into a multitude of job opportunities.

You can really put your personality and #Drama to great use working in television. The entire process from the first audition to the day of the shoot is a fast-paced adventure full of change. Television incorporates your improvisation and memorization skills from dance with your flexibility as an actor.

The audition process for dancing on TV is unique. While you may have to endure big cattle calls for some of the reality-based dance shows, most scripted shows hold smaller auditions that are focused on casting specific parts. Generally, your agent will call or e-mail you with details of the TV show you are auditioning for (isn't that *sooo* #Hollywood?). Your agent will also send you a breakdown* of the part, which you should study carefully so you show up to the audition prepared! This is the prime time to use your acting training. Dress the part. Even if you don't have lines, create an interesting character. Are you a bunhead or a B-boy? Maybe you are a contemporary dancer with an edge. Or is musical theater your style? Use your strengths to add to your vibe, and that energy will come across in your dance performance.

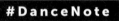

#DanceNote

You don't realize the importance of excellent ballet technique until you find yourself at an audition with a room full of dancers who have it.

If you think texting is fast, just wait until you work on television. The turnaround time is quick. The new episodes that you watch today were most likely shot only a few weeks before airing. When a TV show needs to cast for a dance scene, the casting director will reach out to dance agents with the breakdown. If you are one of the #Lucky dancers that match the breakdown that the scene requires, your agent will call you for the audition.

Although every production has its own unique way of holding auditions, most dance calls involve working with the

---

* A *breakdown* describes a character or role. It includes detailed information on age range, height, hair color, and character backstory. It may also include notes on wardrobe and what to prepare.

choreographer. The choreographer knows exactly what the director is looking for in terms of the scene and will select "favorites." Occasionally you will be called in to improvise for the casting director or director of the episode. Either way, your audition you will most likely be put on tape (think of this like a mobile upload)—only, instead of sharing with friends, the casting director shares with the director and producers. If they *love* what they see, then you get booked!

No matter how long you have been in the business, so much of the film and television process is completely out of the hands of the auditioning performer. Generally, it boils down to the needs of the casting director: Do they look the part? Do they have experience on set? Do they have the acting ability? Are they the right height/weight/hair color/age, etc.? The list goes on and on and on and on, but you get it. It's not personal—it's *typecasting*. You will not fit every type or book every job, but don't let the inevitable rejection stop you from working toward your dream.

The good news is that you control how casting perceives you at the audition, so you *betta* work it out! Do your research. Make sure you are informed about the show and the part for which you are auditioning. Familiarize yourself with the choreographer's previous work. During the audition, have fun with the story, and bring your character to life within the boundaries set by the choreographer. Doing your homework doubles your chances of being considered for the job. Everyone in this industry wants to work with people who know how to get their job done.

Brace yourself. There will be auditions when you get cut and you leave feeling like you could be the worst dancer/actor/singer/human on the planet. It's like posting a selfie on

Instagram before remembering that you have a huge zit
on your face. It's embarrassing,
but it happens to everyone.
No matter how long you have
been in the business or how
great people think you are, we
are only human. The important

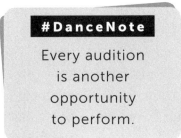

thing is to delete the moment and move on. We never do as
badly as we think we did, and we are never as spectacular as we
think we were. Besides, sometimes you will book the job simply
because you look the part.

My favorite audition was for an episode of *Cold Case*
that centered on a murder backstage at a community theater. My agent had said that they were looking
for dancers with strong acting skills to portray the
community-theater actors. This was my moment to
"Gleek" out!

I showed up to the audition in full character, wearing an outfit so shameless it would have made Lady
Gaga laugh out loud. And that was only the beginning.
I spent the entire audition purposefully counting the
music and singing off-key when I wasn't busy pretend-
ing to forget the choreography.

When it was time to go on camera for the director,
I stated my name in character, and added a wacky (and
phony) story about my experience in community theater, similar to a sketch Justin Timberlake might do on
Saturday Night Live.

The audition was like getting to ride my favorite
roller coaster over and over again without waiting in

line. I booked the job, and I'm pleased to report that the entire process was equally as delightful. The best part is, I'm still getting residual payments for it. Wait until I tell you more about these magical checks that show up in your mailbox when you least expect it.

#Film

If you think working on the small screen sounds mind-blowing, wait until I tell you about the silver screen. Honestly, what's more outrageous than seeing your face plastered fifty-feet high next to one of your favorite movie stars? Well, I'm sure getting paid like

On the set of *Cold Case* with fabulous choreographer Travis Payne (who choreographed for Michael Jackson!) and a killer cast: Stacy Walker, Aisha Francis, Tyce Diorio, Nancy O'Meara, Rita Maye Bland, Gigi Hunter, Anthony Marciona, and Yvette Tucker

a celebrity would be nice, but dancing with them is still worth celebrating. Auditioning and working as a dancer in a movie can be similar to working on a television show. Once again, the casting director's prime objective is to find dancers that look the part and get the job done.

> **#DanceNote**
>
> Well-rounded dancers acknowledge their limitations and strike a balance between improving the things they can do and finding ways around the things they can't.

The noticeable difference between working on film and working on television is the amount of time and money that is invested. The locations, sets, wardrobe, hair and makeup, craft services, background talent, and crew must be orchestrated so that everything stays on schedule. Throw in a #Fabulous production number with a choreographer, her sassy assistant, and forty-five dancers, and you can imagine how many obstacles can arise.

It takes more energy to set up one shot for a movie than it does to do a swan lift with Abby Lee Miller as your dance partner. For each scene, the location has to be locked down; the set has to be lit; the actors, dancers, and background must go through wardrobe, hair, and makeup; the dialogue is blocked; and the camera shots are rehearsed before the director ever calls "Action!"

Big changes mean production losses in terms of time and money, so bring your A game to the set each and every day. Learn to adapt without rehearsal. Be prepared to work with new partners, adjust spatially, and improvise. On the off chance

On the set of *Jackass Number Two* with my talented dance-partner-turned-diva-choreographer, Krista Miller (Google her daughter, YouTube sensation Autumn Miller. #Fierce!)

that the choreography is not working, the director is counting on every person involved to rise to the occasion.

#WhatToExpectOnSet

Booking the job is only half the battle. Once you have the part, you have to keep it! Film and television are multibillion-dollar industries, and no one—I repeat, *no one*—has the time or energy for inappropriate behavior on set. Just ask Lindsay Lohan. No matter how talented or brilliant you know you are, leave your diva at the door. This isn't fifth-period Spanish class, so make sure you show up to all of your rehearsals, costume fittings, and call times *on* time. *On time* means warmed up and ready to go at least fifteen minutes early. Allow plenty of time for parking and that accident blocking five lanes of traffic on the 405.*

> **#DanceNote**
>
> Technique is the key to enjoying a long career. But your ability as a performer to tell a story is the *only* way you'll have a career.

The rehearsal process varies from job to job; however, the majority of the work that you will do as a dancer in LA will be spent on a set. On larger movies and music videos you will likely rehearse at a dance studio or on a soundstage. Be prepared to learn a lot of choreography fast and furiously. Then, be prepared to relearn new choreography on the shoot days. (It's the same story every time—the choreographer has one idea, and the director has another! Guess who wins.)

Be ready for anything. The more you accept that everything is out of your control, the easier it will be for you to have fun. You may have auditioned to dance in a big musical-theater number, and on the day of the shoot you might end up riding a bike in the background. Go with the flow.

---

* It takes at least an hour to get anywhere in LA.

Keep in mind that you may book the job, rehearse the scene, shoot the movie, and realize that the entire scene has been cut from the film. Or, *worse*, you might get the job and be replaced with a new set of dancers because the director "didn't like the vibe." It happens. This industry is very unpredictable; it's simultaneously an exciting adventure and upsetting process. I'm going to repeat myself like an eighty-year-old grandma: You cannot take things personally in LA. You just have to move on to the next opportunity.

Make sure you have a point of contact for every project you are working on. In some instances, it will be the choreographer; on other projects, you may check in with an assistant director (AD) or a production assistant (PA). I urge you to keep track of the people you work with on every project—from the casting director to the camera operator. The more you work in LA, the more you will discover how small the entertainment industry is. You will work with the same people again.

> In one of my sassier moments (and early on in my career), I was lucky enough to book a big TV commercial. I arrived bright and early and reported straight to hair and makeup. I'm not sure if it was my lack of Starbucks or maturity, but I definitely started off on the wrong foot with my hairstylist.
>
> In an effort to be "funny" (and without caffeine) at five o'clock in the morning, I made a joke about his male-pattern baldness. "I'd like to keep mine a little longer on the top, please," I snorted as I plopped down in the chair. He didn't laugh. I left his chair with a hairdo that would make the Hair Don't list in *US Weekly* and makeup that rivaled Ronald McDonald's. What's worse,

the stylist happened to be good friends with the wardrobe supervisor. Guess who I was off to see next?

The costumer allowed me two options: one involved see-through mesh; the other looked like something CeeLo Green would wear to a funeral. Both were too small.

What started out as my trying to be funny on set turned into my looking like a *fool* on national TV. The good news is that I worked with the same hairstylist on another project a few months later. To my delight, he remembered me, and my hair suffered for my wisecrack one more time!

It takes a team larger than Beyoncé and Jay-Z's entourage to make a movie. Everyone from the crew to the accountant who cuts your check is equally essential in this industry. If you want to make it in Hollywood, be the person everyone wants to work with. Producers, directors, and choreographers prefer to hire someone they have used before and trust rather than risk hiring someone who isn't professional. It is tough to break in, so once you have, keep that door open!

The rehearsal process is long, and shooting days are even longer. You will sit around for hours waiting to be called to set, and then you will stand around forever while the crew resets the lights. You will be expected to dance at a moment's notice. Stay warm, and keep that positive attitude. Don't turn into Katherine from *The Vampire Diaries*!

Make friends on every set, and put that networking to good use. Bring a book and a bag of healthy snacks that will provide you with energy to get through the long days. Unless you plan on spending twice as much time in the gym, I would make smart choices when visiting the craft-service table* (which is provided on all television and movie sets), because that dough-nut that seems like a good idea during the fourteenth-hour meal penalty will not be your friend tomorrow.

#Residuals

I like to think of residual payments as special little rewards that magically appear in the mail when you least expect money and *need* it the most. It's like finding $200 in the back pocket of a pair of jeans you haven't worn in three years. While you should never count on residual payments as a steady source of income, if you work often enough, residual payments will be a nice supplement.

Residuals are paid to performers who work on union television, film, and commercial projects as compensation for continuing to use your performance. These payments are on top of your original paycheck. Though times are changing with more Internet-based programming and general buyouts (when you receive a negotiated onetime payment for the project without residuals), there is a specific formula no one but the SAG-AFTRA accountants understand. The best part is that you will receive residuals for as long as the project airs anywhere in the world. Who cares if the amounts get smaller

---

* *Craft services* is a delicious assortment of gourmet and junk food that is available on set all day and night for talent and crew. Make no mistake, the crew can eat as much as they want and *never* gain weight, because they are engaged in hard physical labor all day. The same is not true for actors. You have been warned.

as time goes on? You might still be making money for a job you worked ten years ago.

Whether you want to strike a pose on stage with Madonna (please tell me you didn't have to Google Madonna) or dance next to your favorite celeb in a blockbuster movie, Los Angeles is the place to be and be seen. Now that you have done some homework, I encourage you to practice your best red-carpet strut for your star-studded premieres to come!

Intermission

#DealingWithDivas

Every dancer will eventually face off against a spirit-crushing, nasty, bitter, jaded, tired, overworked, underpaid choreographer who has it out for someone. I've been the victim of this egomaniacal monster several times throughout my career. I'd *like* to tell you that dealing with these diabolic creatures gets easier as you become more established. Sadly, it never does. I present a Tale of Three Divas.

#BadTeacher

During my first year on scholarship at Giordano Dance Chicago, our usual ballet mistress was on leave. For three weeks we were blessed with a less-than-friendly substitute, who had it out for me. One day, during a tendu combination at the barre, she asked me to stand in croisé. In a momentary fit of panic, I stood frozen in front of all my peers, unable to recall which way to

face. Rather than help-
ing me, this particularly
difficult diva laughed
and directed me to a
poster outside of the
dance studio. She con-
tinued to further beat
me down for no other

#DanceNote

A tendu will always
lead you to a
stronger pointe
of view!

reason than to appease her own lack of professional
experience, challenging my future as a dancer. I was
young, and instead of pulling her aside after class to tell
her that my feelings were hurt, I decided to attack back
in the middle of class. I released a rapid-fire round of
insults that had her head spinning so fast her bun fell
out. For the first time in weeks, she was speechless. As
grateful as I was to have rendered her silent, it occurred
to me that, despite her destructive and demeaning dis-
position, I was no better than she. I had worked harder
than ever during the time she was our ballet teacher
just to prove her wrong about me—not necessarily the
right reason, but I'd been determined to rise above her
negative energy. For the first time in my life, I accepted
that I could learn something from even the worst situ-
ations. That ballet battle caused both of us to behave
out of line in front of our colleagues. It was one dance I
never wanted to perform again!

#BadChoreographer

Later in my career, I witnessed a fellow dancer get
massacred by a choreographer who found it more

appealing to scream than clearly articulate direction. We had been rehearsing the same choreography for several days, and while I was also disappointed that my castmate couldn't remember his blocking, I was frustrated that our "leader" was insulting another performer in our ensemble, thus bringing down the morale of our entire show. This particular choreographer is now "*So You Think You Can* famous," and I have many friends who have fallen prey to the beast. What I will always remember is how I held my tongue and watched as the producer of the show stormed in and swiftly reminded our evil genius that they were hired to choreograph, not bully our cast, and that if the problem continued they would be fired. I was elated to hear that our boss wasn't going to tolerate abusive behavior regardless of how brilliant or "important" this choreographer was.

> **#DanceNote**
>
> Dancers who develop their skills as choreographers and teachers have more opportunities in their careers.

#BadCollaborator

Recently, I cochoreographed a project with a woman who enjoyed power more than a high school cheerleader running for senior class president. She had no jurisdiction over my position with the company but continued to try to manipulate and intimidate me. After one particularly nasty rehearsal (where she fought with me in front of our cast), I went to our producer and expressed my concerns in an effort to resolve the differences with my coworker in a respectful and professional manner. We met in a conference room, where she continued to insult my position and ability in front of our boss. I turned to her and calmly said, "I was hired by this company—not by you—because of my extensive background and ability. I didn't ask for your opinion, nor do I care if you think I'm qualified. I don't appreciate the way that you communicate to our cast or with me. I believe that there is a more respectful way to encourage artists, and, although you have spent the majority of your career teaching others, I assure you I am just as proficient at teaching without the need for nasty remarks." Following that meeting (and most certainly as payback to me), she grew increasingly horrid to our cast. I did my best to assure each of the dancers how pleased I was with their hard work, creativity, and positive energy. Even though I enjoyed working with my cast, my "partner's" negative energy had convinced me to not return for another contract.

> **#DanceNote**
>
> The entertainment industry implies that success as an artist is defined by money and fame. I choose to believe that success is defined by waking up each day in pursuit of fulfilling your greatest dreams.

There will always be people unwilling to set their egos aside for the betterment of the project. Creative people with strong personalities can often be emotional, but that doesn't mean that they should belittle you. Instead of getting upset when your turn in that particularly uncomfortable spotlight comes, remember to stay calm and focus on doing what you love. You are not responsible for other people's negative energy. As dancers, we are usually collaborative people. We won't always love the choreography or the person choreographing it, but we can always dare ourselves to search for the creative lesson and grow from it.

"God, I Hope I Get It"

I F YOU are as dedicated to your career as Kurt or Rachel from *Glee*, then my guess is that you have already had the opportunity to audition for a part or even perform in a school play, Nutcracker ballet, recital, or dance team. (If not, add the movies *First Position*, *Bring It On*, and *Every Little Step* to your Netflix queue ASAP for instant industry research!) As over the top and clichéd as a movie montage can be, the audition process can be just as ridiculous. Never fear: just like your favorite movie moment, your dance career can have a happy ending if you utilize the information provided here.

#Agents

Everybody has an agent, right? Well, not exactly. Though it's a goal for most dancers who want to work, signing with an agent takes time. Before we cover that, it's important to understand the role of agents and how they work for you.

An agent connects clients with casting and is on the phone more than a teenage girl going through a #Major breakup. Agents spend their days talking to casting directors, choreographers, and producers to learn about upcoming projects and to pitch any clients who fit the desired breakdowns. Hit *pause* on iTunes, and get ready to pin this piece of advice: Your. Agent. Cannot. Get. You. The. Job. They open doors, but it's up to you to take advantage of the space inside the room! You might be the next Selena Gomez if you continuously build your talent, introduce yourself to the working choreographers (by taking classes), and develop your own #Brand. Be creative and fearless. Collaborating with other dancers and producing your own dance projects provide your representation something to talk about when they're on the phone pitching you. The more outgoing and creative you are, the more chances your agent has to get you seen. Now more than ever, young artists harness social media and YouTube to expand their visibility. Don't be lazy and wait for somebody else to "make you a star," or your fairytale fantasy will not be *Enchanted*!

When you book the job, your agent will negotiate your contract and handle all of the aspects of your booking—such as corresponding your rehearsal schedule, arranging costume fittings, and coordinating travel if necessary. For all of this valuable work, your agent pockets an industry standard 10 percent of your earnings* (20 percent on some nonunion jobs). Your agent only makes money when you do, which is a big motivating factor for everyone involved. Reputable agents never ask for money up front. If they do, run out the door and never go back!

---

* I know 10 percent sounds like a lot of money, but you would have a lot less if you didn't get the job. Ninety percent of something is better than 100 percent of nothing!

The average dance agency represents hundreds of talented clients. Like you, each client thinks he is the next Travis Wall. Obviously the agent does too, or she wouldn't waste energy pitching clients for jobs. So, unless you failed fourth-period math class, you can add up the number of odds against you. Not everyone can book every job, so you have to get out there and hustle. Take the classes with the choreographers your agent recommends. Attend industry showcases, and network. Make sure that everyone in the dance scene knows that you are talented and ready to work. Now aren't you glad you took Marguerite Derricks's class at The Edge and gave them something to talk about?

I know what you are thinking: Enough advice, already; you sound like my ballet teacher! How do I get an agent?

Signing with an agent can be more challenging than sitting through *Titanic* without a box of tissues. In the bigger markets like Los Angeles and New York, most of the dance agencies hold general auditions throughout the year. They will post a call with all of the major industry trade papers and websites. At the open call you will be taught several combinations and styles of choreography. If they like what they see, they'll sign you to their roster. (Never fear! For all of you slackers I've compiled a list of the best dance agencies and websites

> **#DanceNote**
>
> Making it as a professional dancer requires every ounce of passion, training, and hard work you have in you. It also means facing rejection on a daily basis. Once you can acknowledge this, release it and get back into ballet class!

in the Encore.) Agents also attend dance classes and workshops to scout for new talent. Occasionally they will ask choreographers for their recommendations. The best way to get an agent is to be prepared as a dancer and know your limitations.

Not signing with an agent right away doesn't mean you won't work as a dancer. In fact, several resources and websites (also in the Encore) post auditions for union and nonunion dancers every day. As I mentioned earlier, Broadway shows have required union calls for chorus dancers, and those auditions can be found on the Actors' Equity Association website.*

Once you book your first professional job, you can send a picture and résumé to all of the dance agents in your city asking them for a meeting. You might also make friends with the other dancers you are working with and ask them to introduce you to their agents. Don't be shy. It's a small world with plenty of room for more than one dancer. Dancers who help each other get jobs continue to work themselves! Think of it like an alliance in *The Hunger Games. You* control your career. If you want to work, get out there and look for jobs.

> **#DanceNote**
>
> Expand your knowledge of dance! Study the masters online. You can start by Googling Martha Graham, Bob Fosse, George Balanchine, and Alvin Ailey.

---

* Check out Equity's audition postings at http://www.actorsequity.org/CastingCall/castingcallhome.asp.

#Picture

Thanks to Instagram, you are already a fashionista who knows how to pose in front of the camera. Keep working those skills by practicing different reactions and looks that sync with your personality. Along with your best smiling commercial shot and your most menacing theatrical glare, your agents may want additional pictures that show off your skill and how you come across as a dancer. Keep in mind that your picture and résumé are a calling card to everyone in the industry. Make sure your headshot looks like you, not some Photoshopped *In Touch Weekly* cover of Jennifer Lawrence!

When you have an agent, listen to him! He knows the market and where you will fit in. If you aren't working with an agent, just remember to stay true to who you are on the inside and make sure that translates in your picture. As a rule, don't wear too much makeup. You should look like *you* on your best day. Also be careful to not overstyle yourself. Those earrings might be fun at the club but aren't appropriate in a headshot. You want the focus to be on you, not your Carrie Bradshaw flair! Before you shoot with the photographer, make sure you feel confident. Ask all of your questions up front, and, above all else, have fun on the day of the shoot. (This also means you can't party like a rock star the night before!)

#Résumé

Building an impressive résumé to attach on the back of your eight-by-ten headshot is tough if you don't have a lot of experience. Never fear—everyone starts out the same way! Each agency provides a template for how they'd like your résumé to look. The most important thing to include is your name and contact information. Do not put your address or social security number on the résumé, unless you want some imposter stealing your information and living your life for you. When starting out, it's okay to include competitions and school shows along with your training and any job experience. As you begin to work as a professional, you can remove the outdated information and replace it with those awesome gigs! Never lie on your résumé. During the audition process you may be asked about a specific job that you have listed. You don't want to be a *Pretty Little Liar*, so don't get caught up in that #Drama. If you don't have an agent, check out my website for an idea of what your résumé should look like.*

#Reel

Originally a tool for actors and directors in Hollywood, the reel is becoming an industry standard for dancers. Similar to a trailer for a summer blockbuster movie, a reel highlights your best work. In a perfect world, your reel should show off your impressive style and range. Include live concerts, company work, commercials—even that self-produced dance video going viral on YouTube! Add anything that shows the choreographer or producer watching how you look and perform on film. You are a product of the twenty-first century, right? So why not incorporate the user-friendly editing technology (like iMovie) to change up your reel, add your favorite new songs, and keep people guessing? The more hands-on you are with every aspect of your career, the greater the opportunity for work. The best

---

*You can find my résumé at http://www.matthewshaffer.com/.

way to learn about the industry is to learn the basics of every aspect of the industry. As I mentioned in earlier chapters, you will most likely begin your career taking jobs that pay less (and are perhaps nonunion). The advantage is that these jobs make for strong reel-building footage. Just like your pictures and résumé, you should continue to reimagine your reel. Your agent will submit this "tape" to casting directors, producers, and industry professionals who are interested in booking you for work, so keep it fresh and entertaining! After all, it's a digital calling card that will lead you to great success. For *reelz*!

#Website

Undoubtedly you have a Facebook page and Twitter and Instagram accounts, and you understand how major it is to be active in building your brand via social media. Now it's time to tackle your own website (if you haven't already)! Creating a website further establishes your brand, personality, and point of view. With your own website, you can easily organize your headshots, résumé, reel, and blog and connect all of your social-media accounts. It's a killer way to make online introductions! E-mail a link of your site to potential employers, and in just one click they can have instant access to your media! There are dozens of *free* website builders online, and if you do it yourself you can keep it as current as Nicki Minaj's hairstyles.

> **#DanceNote**
>
> The fastest way to achieve success in the dance industry is at the ballet barre.

#Unions

In order to work on television, film, and Broadway, you will have to join one or more of the performers' unions. The unions were established to enforce safe working conditions, negotiate fair pay with producers, and ensure that each member has a voice. The fee to join each of these unions varies. Members pay annual dues based on the amount of money earned in each union. Once you are a member, you are protected as a professional.

You can only join a union when you book a union job. In order to audition for union jobs, however, you have to be in the union. Figuring out how to join a union can be more complicated than following the storyline of *Inception*! Here's what I can tell you: Every working dancer eventually finds a way into the union. You just keep working until you book a job that requires you to join. Four major unions cover the working conditions and contracts for dancers:

1. **The Screen Actors Guild–American Federation of Television and Radio Artist (SAG-AFTRA)** covers the jurisdiction for most television and film work, including commercials, corporate films, and music videos.*

2. **The Actors' Equity Association (AEA)** handles Broadway and musical-theater performers.†

3. **The American Guild of Variety Artists (AGVA)** represents dancers in theme parks and larger theatrical productions.‡

4. **The American Guild of Musical Artists (AGMA)** protects dancers working in ballet and concert-dance companies.§

---

* You can find SAG-AFTRA online at http://www.sagaftra.org/.

† You can find the AEA online at http://www.actorsequity.org/.

‡ You can find AVGA online at http://www.agvausa.com/.

§ You can find AGMA online at http://www.musicalartists.org/.

Once you are in the union, you can no longer take non-union work. There is twice as much nonunion work nowadays, so while you might make more money on a union gig, you will most likely work more if you are nonunion. All of this will make more sense once you are faced with the option. The key is to decide how long you want to work nonunion jobs to build experience and credits on your résumé before auditioning for jobs that are union only.

#Show(Business)

A long and successful career stems from understanding and accepting that you are not *just* a dancer or any other creative variation (i.e., "dancer who sings," "actor who dances," and so on). You are a business and a brand. Listen to the advice and feedback that your agents and industry pros offer. As your own boss, you set the tone for your style and marketing.

Dancers who continue to explore their creative voices maintain career longevity. They evolve as artists and keep their images current. Successful dancers know themselves from the inside out, including their limitations, shortcomings, and talents and how others perceive them in the industry. It's not about knowing where you fit in; it's about knowing where you stand out among the best.

Be like Elle Woods in *Legally Blonde*, and get involved in dance-related industry functions and meetings to learn what other successful performers are working on. As you tackle bigger projects, you will develop relationships with industry insiders with whom you can collaborate. Allies in the entertainment business are always assets. Not everyone will be eager to help you advance, so take your time establishing meaningful friendships. There is a learning curve, but you will find out very quickly which jobs and projects to fight for. Trust your instincts, and know the demographic in which you best fit.

As for contracts, *don't* sign anything until you have had a second person look it over (preferably an agent or lawyer). If you don't have an agent and can't afford a lawyer, your parents, a friend, or another family member may always know someone who can help. There are also organizations and resources that are able to help you for free, especially through your union #GoodReasonToJoin. Any legitimate job will give you the opportunity to read a contract entirely and ask questions. If someone forces you to sign on the dotted line before you have had a professional look it over, *run away* faster than Forrest Gump! You will become more familiar with general contracts and basic rules for dancers as you continue to work.

#TheAudition

Here's the scoop: Every audition is a unique process that involves a huge creative team and a lot of "important" people. You might be called into a big room with hundreds of dancers (cattle calls #Gross!). It might be an agent call with forty dancers. Or you may find yourself in a small casting office with two other performers who look just like you.

> I was relaxing on my couch at home watching *American Idol* when I got a last-minute call from my agent to audition for the Disney XD show *Kickin' It.* Sweet! I love the rush of an unexpected opportunity.
>
> It was already nearly 10 P.M., and I had to learn a piece of choreography online and be ready to audition the next morning at nine. The previous actor hadn't

worked out, so if I booked the part, I would go straight into wardrobe and shoot later that day!

The morning of the audition, I sized up the four other guys who were also auditioning as I signed in. I was ready for *war*. One by one, my targets were called into a small room with the casting director. As each dancer exited the room, I got more excited for

> **#DanceNote**
>
> Every audition is a new chance to network and meet new people. Make a positive first impression!

the dance off. I knew I was perfect for the part; now I just had to convince the director!

When they called my name, I walked in like I was John Travolta (think *Stayin' Alive*, not *Hairspray*), and I nailed the dance. Afterward, the director asked me to improvise my "best strut" from one side of the shoe-box sized room to the other. When I finished, the director said, "Great," whispered something in the casting director's ear, and walked out of the room. Deflated that he didn't worship me like the dance genius I thought I was, I rushed out and was ready to crawl back to my car.

Moments from dropping to my knees to begin my (oh-so-subtle) sneak-out, the casting director stopped me and led me back to her office. With a big smile on her face, she said, "We want to hire you. But we'd like to wait until the other guys leave the studio before we send you to wardrobe."

> Just like that, I booked the job! I went through
> wardrobe and hair and makeup, and in less than two
> hours I was working on the set! It was #Awesome.

Regardless of the process, you have to do your job to book the job! That means research. Find out what the creative team wants before the audition. If they want wholesome, clean-cut Disney dancers, don't go in looking like you just walked off of the set of *Burlesque*. You have to dress and act the part. I'm not saying you should pretend to be someone you're not. Insincerity or fakeness often comes across as just bad acting. Instead, rely on the skills you hone in acting class. You *are* in acting class right? Pull from your own experiences in life. Be confident, and, if nothing else, have fun! It's okay to take chances as long as you are always honest in your delivery. Stay true to you, and celebrate your individuality.

If a casting director or choreographer has called you in before, remind him how he knows you. Also try to recall the notes from the last time you auditioned. If they love your dance ability but didn't like your look, change it up.

Like your world-history teacher said, "Grab a highlighter; you're gonna want to remember this!" I strongly urge you to keep a book of all the auditions and jobs you've worked. I print out the e-mail for each project and write all of my notes on it. I keep track of the names of everyone I worked with and what notes or advice they gave me.* (This includes funny stories or things that made them laugh—anything that I can reference the

---

* If you are an overachiever like me, take advantage of twenty-first-century technology to keep track of everything on your iPhone. That way all of those important names, notes, and connections are always in the palm of your hand.

next time we meet.) This is a business that involves networking. In order to stay connected, you have to recall the details.

Assuming the *E! True Hollywood Story* is accurate, Jennifer Lopez started off as a dancer just like you and me! She trained in New York City and worked her way from a dancer on *In Living Color* to a multimillion-dollar box office #Brand! Regardless of whether you think she's a great singer, actor, or dancer, it's undeniable that Jenny from the Block exploited her assets before anyone could use them against her. She made being J.Lo *hot*.

#DanceNote

If your arabesque line isn't behind you with your hips square, then it's probably in second position—and second position is *second*-besque!

I admire Jennifer's drive, unique style, and creativity. She proves that every dancer out there can manifest their dreams if they commit to cultivating their connections, exploring new ventures, and refining their voice. *Werk* it out!

Time to Take
the Grand Jeté

HOPEFULLY YOU have absorbed the information provided in the previous chapters better than the notes you took in fourth-period math class, and you are ready to select a location to begin your first dance away from home.

You wouldn't move to Phoenix if you were an aspiring snowboarder, just like you probably wouldn't consider living in Seattle if you hate the rain.

If the marquees and neon lights of Broadway are flashing your name, New York is the place for you. Attending a university near the city is one way to transition from high school to life on the Great White Way. While in school, you can enjoy the luxuries New York has to offer. Take professional classes, audition for Broadway shows, and network within the theater community. In the meantime, you are saving money on rent, expanding your education, and building up a group of friends, all of which are priceless in a city like New York.

If you decide against four more years of school but would still like to move to New York, fear not. Harness your training as a dancer, and take the leap.

> #DanceNote
>
> Set aside fifteen minutes a day for creative writing or journaling. A dancer who knows who they are emotionally will soar creatively.

On July 2, 1999, I flew from Chicago O'Hare to La Guardia Airport with one mission: become a star! Thanks to the many summers I'd spent in New York sneaking out of theater camps for a wild adventure, I considered myself an expert on the city. As soon as the airplane touched down, I was to discover just how wrong I had been.

Fortunately, I was making the move with a friend. Unfortunately, she was as oblivious as Karen Smith in *Mean Girls*.

It had never occurred to either of us to devise a plan before we left Chicago. Neither had it ever occurred to us that we'd be lost in Long Island, drenched in a sudden downpour, stuck sleeping on a friend's sofa in a one-bedroom apartment shared with three other roommates who were as happy to have us there as they were delighted with the roaches that infested the kitchen, and finally held up at gunpoint on a fifty-minute train ride to Brooklyn. If this was "making it" in the Big Apple, then count me out.

STEP ONE: find an apartment. After a full week of pounding the pavement with no luck and no more

time, we decided to sacrifice our food money to buy
an "exclusive apartment listing" from a sketchy ad we'd
seen in the *New York Times*. Forty phone calls and
twenty listings later, we found an apartment in a prime
area of the Upper West Side. After negotiating our rent
with the shady building manager (who made Lord
Voldemort look like Tinker Bell), we had our very own
two-hundred-square-foot apartment with no kitchen,
and it only cost us four *thousand* dollars up front.

Sounds as scary as *Final Destination*, right? Well, it was. It was
also a thrilling journey full of growth and self-discovery—very
similar to a Lifetime movie.

Moving to a new city can be overwhelming for anyone, but the
odds in favor of a smooth transition increase if you do some planning. Before you pack your bags and jump on an airplane, decide
which field of dance appeals to you. While you can pursue almost
any medium of dance anywhere nowadays, New York makes more
sense for a dancer who wants to do musical theater and perform
on Broadway. Los Angeles seems more appropriate for a dancer
who wants to work on film and television, while innovators of
concert dance should flock to Chicago or New York. Naturally,
you can change your mind about your career path as many times
as popular kids in middle school change BFFs. Still, it's always nice
to have a general plan of attack.

#Housing

Your first priority is a roof over your head. You want to find a safe,
affordable home close to where you will be working, rehearsing,
and auditioning. In most cases, dancers have to work late hours,

so make sure you live in an area where you feel safe walking to the train or your car.

Ask yourself questions when considering an apartment: Do I have enough money saved to pay first and last month's rent *and* a security deposit? Will I be able to afford the rent on my budget? Is this apartment near a place I can work, where I will rehearse, a grocery store, and inexpensive nightlife? Are there roommates? If necessary, could I accommodate a roommate or sublet the apartment while I'm on tour? (Roommates can become good friends if you're lucky or bitter enemies if you don't get along.)

Subletting allows you to keep the apartment in your name while renting it out to other people for short periods of time. (Think of it as renting your fabulous sunglasses to someone else while you are not wearing them.) Since finding an apartment costs so much money, you don't want to start the process over every time you leave town for work. Always check with your landlord and the city housing authority to confirm if subletting is legal. Otherwise you will get stuck paying for rent even if you are not home!

The cool thing is, subletting works both ways. (Think of it as renting fabulous sunglasses from someone else who isn't wearing them.) It's an outstanding way to check out a city before you move. There are plenty of places that you can find sublets available online, but the bulletin board at the local dance studio is a brilliant place to start.

#FACT: finding an apartment is tougher than preparing for the SATs! Get ready to pound the pavement. Search online, through newspapers, and on message boards at dance studios in the area. Meet with people during the day only, and tell a friend or coworker where you are going before each meeting. Not everyone is as nice or trustworthy as you think. And even if you are more desperate to find a place than Amanda Bynes is for another comeback, *never* sign a lease or exchange money until you know what you are signing up for!

#GetAJob

Once you have your living situation under control, the next step is survival. That shoebox of an apartment you share with two dancers you just met at an audition comes with a hefty price tag. Concentrate on finding a job that pays for your bills and classes, lets you off for auditions, and hopefully leaves you some money to eat. (I recommend Top Ramen and almonds.)

The two Rs—retail and restaurants—make great survival jobs. The hours are flexible, the pay is reasonable, and, chances are, they will be more accommodating with unexpected shift changes.

During your senior year of high school or college, consider applying for a job with a company that has a location in the city you plan on moving to. A job at the Gap, Pottery Barn, Barnes & Noble, or a restaurant chain such as Olive Garden, T.G.I. Friday's, or Applebee's can be an excellent way to save money for your move and provide a job when you reach your new destination! *Plus*, you are guaranteed to have a fierce wardrobe or a nice warm meal.

My first year away from home, I was desperate for money. I was tired of eating instant mashed potatoes covered in ketchup from packets that I'd "borrowed" from the McDonald's on my way home from rehearsal. (Don't judge me; it was cheap, and I was #Broke.) I decided to get a job working as a host at a popular breakfast restaurant in Chicago.

Between gym workouts, rehearsals, and classes, I could only work two shifts a week in order to make ends meet. But the job provided so much more than a paycheck. I met some of my best friends working there, and I got to eat a free meal on every shift I worked. They were the only real meals I ate for over six months. I was lucky to have that job.

Regardless of where you end up working, keep in mind that the job is for survival. Too often newcomers get so wrapped up in their life at work that they forget why they moved to a new city in the first place. Pursuing your career as a performer comes first. Don't make a habit of hanging out after your shift drinking and socializing with your coworkers. An active social life is wonderful, but if you spend more time drinking away your hard-earned money than working toward your professional goals, that survival job just became the job that killed your dream.

> **#DanceNote**
>
> Balancing a successful career requires disciplined scheduling: work, training, creative time, sleep, and social activities.

#RockYourCity

You decorated your apartment with the finest secondhand furniture Craigslist had to offer, you are taking classes and networking, and you've locked down the perfect survival job. Now it's time to rock out in your city. You picked the prime location for a reason, so get out there and enjoy what it has to offer!

Most artists get so engrossed in their training that they forget to incorporate their surroundings for creative inspiration. In the course of my career, I've had the privilege of living in New York, Chicago, and Los Angeles. I've also explored cities in forty-nine of the fifty states and many European countries (thanks to several years on tour). Take it from me—an adventure awaits everywhere you land!

I never miss an opportunity to strike an Instagram #DancePose—this while working in New York City.

The easiest way to introduce yourself to a new city is with the help of new friends. Instead of wasting your next day off sleeping in like a #Slacker, plan a fun scavenger hunt around the city. Pick a few destinations that don't cost a lot of money, and learn about the culture. If you snap a cool dance shot in each new setting and post it online, you're sharing your creative adventure and building your #Brand at the same time! And did you know that most museums offer free days and student discounts?

#FavoriteAdventuresNYC

Exploring the American Museum of Natural History, window shopping on Fifth Avenue, watching the sunset from the Boat Basin Café on the Upper West Side, walking through Central Park, journaling at Lincoln Center, devouring a delicious hotdog from Gray's Papaya, sipping a hot cappuccino down in SoHo, enjoying dinner on Ninth Avenue at Arriba Arriba, and seeing a Broadway show (thanks to inexpensive tickets from TKTS in Times Square).

#FavoriteAdventuresChicago

Eating peanuts while cheering on the Cubs at Wrigley Field, laughing through an evening of side-splitting humor at the Second City, riding the Ferris wheel at Navy Pier, enjoying a movie and beer at the Brew & View (for those who are old enough), strolling around the lake for inspiration, organizing a pub crawl down Rush Street, exploring the Taste of Chicago (an outdoor food and music festival), planning a trip to Shedd Aquarium, savoring every last bite of the *best* deep-dish pizza you will ever eat at Uno Chicago Grill (a.k.a. Uno's), and, *of course*, catching every concert-dance

There's always time to get a leg up in Times Square!

performance from River North Dance Chicago, Giordano Dance Chicago, and Hubbard Street Dance Chicago!

#FavoriteAdventuresLosAngeles

Releasing stress and enjoying the sun at the beach; hiking and networking the hills of Runyon Canyon; exploring Griffith Observatory; attending *free* jazz nights at the Los Angeles

#ChoreographEverywhere with fellow dancers
Nicholas Pere MacLeod and Devert Hickman

County Museum of Art; window shopping in Beverly Hills, dahling; scoring cheap tickets for the Hollywood Bowl; acting like a tourist along the Hollywood Walk of Fame; stuffing my face with the best French dip sandwich you'll ever eat at Philippe the Original downtown; shopping for affordable soaps and candles in Chinatown; catching shows at the Dorothy Chandler Pavilion; eating for cheap at the Farmers Market; and taking in movies at the ArcLight Hollywood.

Collaborating with friends Jeff Payton, Samuel Lee Roberts,
and Michael McBride from Alvin Ailey #StayCreative

#FavoriteAdventuresOnTour

No matter what city or country I'm in, the first thing I do upon
arriving is find a coffeehouse and strike up a friendly conversation
with the locals while savoring a cup of joe.* It's the fastest way to
hear about all of the "must see/do" activities. A fun way to see the

---

* *Joe* is an old-fashioned way of saying "a cup of coffee." I'm not as old
as you think I am; I just enjoy expanding your vocabulary and paying
homage to my grandpa.

sites and experience the best that each new location has to offer is to take advantage of the city's public transportation system or hop on one of those touristy double-decker busses. I cherish exploring old churches and theaters, scouting through parks, and raising a glass in neighborhood pubs, and I take more photos of the sites than a celebrity stalker. Like any stellar historian, I always keep a journal of my expeditions so that when I'm old and gray I'll have a remarkable memoir of my daring days.

The list of activities in each city could go on forever. The point is that you have to get out there and start your own "must see/do" list. Make sure to check out your local visitors' bureau for additional tips and coupons. And, of course, there's always Google!

> **#DanceNote**
>
> Dancers who take big risks in class have a huge advantage on stage.

Just as a tree doesn't grow without roots, a dancer cannot transition without being grounded, so plant yourself firmly in your new city. Make the most of it! The new bonds you form now will become old friendships that will support you many times over in this industry. If you love to cook, make a healthy dinner and invite a few of your new dance friends over after class. Or plan a movie night and pop a bowl of yummy popcorn. The more you are willing to encounter, the more pages you will fill in your new chapter.

Whether you decide to triumph on stage in New York City, sizzle the screen in Hollywood, electrify the concert-dance scene in Chicago, or soar to new heights elsewhere, build a bond with the city and people that support your dream.

The Inside Scoop

THROUGHOUT my career I have been fortunate to work alongside some of the most brilliant innovators in the industry, and I never missed an opportunity to learn something from each of them. I've shared my stories, sassy advice, and encouragement, but, like any headstrong artist, I bet you need a second opinion. Lucky for you, I've asked the industry's hottest choreographers, directors, casting directors, dancers, and agents to share their insights.

There is no substitute for hard work and dedication to your craft. The choice of being a performer offers a never-ending winding road of learning and discovery. There will be bad times (many rejections) and good times (you're working!). The most exciting thing is what you learn along the way and how you grow over time as a performer and a person. Don't get discouraged. Believe in yourself, and never stop learning!

—JULIE MCDONALD, senior agent and founder,
McDonald Selznick Associates

Stay focused on your dreams, and don't compare your journey to anyone else's. With hard work and determination, everything is possible. Never let anyone tell you, "You can't."

—MARGUERITE DERRICKS, three-time
Emmy Award–winning choreographer

It will take you at least five years to start to book jobs consistently. You have to have the right temperament to wait it out. You have to love dance that much that time isn't a deterrent for you. Breathe, calm yourself, and stay focused. Do your best, and repeat, repeat, repeat. Relationships are key. Remember, people hire who they know over who they don't. That will never change. Being comfortable, for choreographers, is very important, because it frees them up creatively. If they don't know who you are, then you are seen as a risk, and sometimes there is no time for risks. Also, versatility is important. If all you are is proficient in one style, then you considerably cut your chances in regard to how many auditions your agent can actually send you out on. Dancers with more skills are always in demand, just like in any employable environment. I always say, "The more you learn, the more you earn."

—JIM KEITH, president and partner,
The Movement Talent Agency

Challenge yourself to learn a new style or form of dance every six months; education is key. Always do more than is expected of you. It's a simple recipe . . . Hard work pays off.

—NANCY O'MEARA,
TV and film choreographer

Talent is a terrible thing to waste but a wonderful thing to invest in.

> —GROVER DALE, Answers4dancers

An aspiring Broadway performer benefits from strong technique. Learn from the best in the field via classes, workshops, live performance, film, literature, and networking. If your aim is to do musicals, make singing a priority. Even if you're a dancer first, sing every day. This will give you a leg up at Broadway auditions.

> —CRAIG BURNS, CSA, partner and
> casting director, Telsey + Company

Working as a successful dancer isn't necessarily about who you know, but it is hugely reliant on the reputation you create for yourself. Always be true to yourself and genuine, and know that the people you take classes and work with on a daily basis could be the ones hiring you tomorrow.

> —MELISSA SANDVIG, ballerina and choreographer,
> *So You Think You Can Dance*

A career in this business will have ups and downs. I have enjoyed tremendous, life-affirming highs and heartbreaking lows. I make it a practice to remember that I am the same person regardless of where the spotlight falls. My goal is simply to share the power of dance. My worth is determined by me, not by booking a job or by signing with a particular agent. When I remember my goal and stand in my worth, I am happier and more secure and have, surprisingly, booked the jobs that were perfect for me.

> —TRACIE STANFIELD, artistic director,
> Synthesis Dance Project

This cannot be accomplished without self-discipline. You must enjoy the work. Also, 90 percent of the jobs you will get will be from the people you are working with at this very moment. So play well with others!

—SAMUEL LEE ROBERTS, dancer,
Alvin Ailey American Dance Theater

Your future is often determined by your reputation. Even if you are just starting out, those dancing beside you, those teaching you, or those observing you may be the ones, down the road, who might recommend you to someone else or even be the ones offering you a job. Be passionate, committed, and disciplined with respect to your craft, and people notice. Be the person everyone wants to work with. Never close a door.

—JOHN DIETRICH, director and choreographer

One summer I went on over eighty auditions and many times would make it to final callbacks. Despite my efforts, I never booked the job. I was frustrated and disheartened but kept going. I had worked as a Radio City Rockette the previous season and was eligible to audition for a new show they were doing. I booked the gig and met a director that continued to hire me for two more Broadway shows! Had I booked any of the previous shows I would have been out of town and missed the audition. Even after you get cut eighty times, never give up!

—MELISSA FAGAN, Broadway performer

Do not seek the praise and approval of others by which to measure your own esteem. As an artist of any discipline, it is essential to continue creating work in which you believe, and the audience will follow.

—JEFF PAYTON, director and producer, A Group Production

When planning for a big audition, I always say to talent, "Preparation versus expectation." So much of a career path is determined by timing and access, so you have to be ready whenever you are lucky enough to get an opportunity! That means being trained, being focused, and being available— emotionally and physically and technically.

—MICHELLE ZEITLIN, talent manager and producer,
More Zap Productions & Management

Go somewhere to get somewhere. It doesn't come to you; you have to go to it. The more you do it, the better you get; the better you get, you get somewhere. Most of all, can't *is a* can-cer.

—SUSAN QUINN WILLIAMS, college professor
and master teacher

Dance with your brain as well as your body: know your limits, and don't injure yourself.

—TROY GARZA, choreographer,
Saturday Night Live, 1990–1999

Success in the dance industry is based on three components in this order: who you know, what you look like, and dance ability, last. You could be the best dancer in the room, but if you are not well networked, do not know the people you are auditioning for, and do not have the "look" that fits their vision for the project, then it might be tough to book the job. The ability to do ten pirouettes is not going to book you the job. The biggest virtue for a new dancer to LA is patience. You have to remember that all of the dancers that are currently in LA arrived here before you. It is like waiting in line for a roller coaster at an amusement park. All of these people have been waiting in line before you, and it is up to you to figure out how you are going to cut in line and get up to the front. This means networking and socializing within the dance community, cultivating a look that makes you stand out from the crowd, and training in styles that can help broaden your movement vocabulary to make you as versatile of a dancer as possible.

—STEVE CHETELAT, talent representative, Bloc Agency

Every behavior is motivated by a thought; every action is prompted by an attitude. Positive thinking is key; your life is shaped by your thoughts.

—SHANNON MATHER, choreographer,
Dancing with the Stars, Mather Dance Company

The most practical advice I can give to a young, aspiring dancer is to never follow fads, never follow what is trendy. Be an individual, and think for yourself. Make certain you exude positive energy in all that you do, and let that radiance pour forth each and every time you dance. I learned this way of living from the best, Gus Giordano, who was my father and my mentor, and his wisdom has served me well for my entire career.

—NAN GIORDANO, artistic director,
Giordano Dance Chicago

Every dancer needs to be prepared for the opportunities and auditions that come their way. I work with the highest level of dancers, and all of our clients treat each audition, every class, and their peers with respect. They constantly challenge themselves inside and outside of the dance studio and castings. Every moment in class and every audition is a golden opportunity to learn something and grow. Our clients work in many areas of dance and are hired repeatedly—not only due to their talent but also for their positive, creative, dedicated, and passionate reputations. To be a successful dancer, you have to be driven and have the discipline to break boundaries, explore new intentions, and be prepared to constantly work at the foundations of technique.

—LAKEY WOLF, agent, CESD Talent Agency

If it isn't fun, don't do it. Work hard, dedicate your time, and believe you are an incredible performer that has what it takes to shine. If you have faith in yourself, you won't have to worry when it comes to competition; and if you aren't cast at an audition, it is they who have missed a great opportunity.

—SANDRA COYTE, CEO,
Starbound National Talent Competition

Make your own path; don't follow the path that everyone has already danced on. It's easy to wear the same styles, train at the same places, or go to the popular conventions that everyone goes to. Try to be true to yourself and what your strengths are as a dancer. As a parent of a young dancer myself, it is hard not to get caught up in what everyone else is doing, especially with social media today; but be true to what you as an artist do best. Train in all styles, but focus on what you do best!

—KRISTA MILLER, teacher and
choreographer, KBM Talent

Dancers should always remember life is all about the connections you make. Always be sure to thank your master teacher or choreographer and introduce yourself. Make yourself known not only as a wonderful and talented dancer but as a person, too.

—NOELLE PATE PACKETT, administrative and regional director, Starpower National Talent Competition

One of the biggest things you can do to be successful in this industry is to be prepared. Know exactly what you're auditioning for and who the choreographer is, view their past work, and, if possible, take a class with them beforehand. There is no such thing as a dumb dancer, only those that didn't take the right steps to be successful. The entertainment industry can be very hard but also extremely rewarding. Treat it like a job, work hard, and always be prepared.

—KACY COMBS, national director, Revolution Talent Competition

Dance competitions today are a fabulous way to gain experience performing in front of a live audience. The critiques given by the professional judges are priceless in the aid of a dancer's overall development.

—GARY PATE, owner, Starpower Talent Competition

Talent is hitting a target no one else can hit. Vision is hitting a target no one else can see. To be successful in today's arts and entertainment industry, you need talent, but, more important, you need vision and an entrepreneurial spirit to maintain relevance in an ever-changing industry.

—RALPH OPACIC, founder and executive director, Orange County School of the Arts

Dance because you have *to, not because you* want *to. Inspiration comes in all forms and at any moment; be open to receiving it. Dream big, 'cause that's where it all starts.*

—STACEY TOOKEY, choreographer,
So You Think You Can Dance

Most dancers today are so well trained, so just do your very best. Don't stray from who you are. Be true to yourself; remember, life is a dance from one stage to the next. Good luck.

—GRACE WAKEFIELD, owner, Starpower Talent Competition

The keys to success are professionalism, great communication with your agent, being realistic about what kind of performer you are, being prepared for whatever may come down your path, and building strong relationships within the community. My father told me when I moved to Los Angeles that your reputation is everything, and he was right. Protect it. Lastly, be the best you that you can be on each and every day. Every dancer has a different path, so define your own success, and don't compare. We are lucky to experience this journey, but keep in mind it is not for everyone; you will be told no more than yes, and it can be difficult at times. In closing, education is also an important part of the plan so that you have as many options as possible.

—TERRY LINDHOLM, president, Go 2 Talent Agency

You really know you belong on stage when the music begins, the curtain rises, and being on that stage feels more like home than home itself—and you can let your true spirit soar.

—BERNADETTE HILL, ballet mistress and performer,
Royal Academy of Dance, Moulin Rouge Paris, and invited
performer for Her Majesty the Queen in the Royal
Command Performance at the London Palladium

Front row. Center stage. Are you there? I surely never even came close! But, hey, isn't it just a "spot on the floor"? So, enjoy the teamwork within your studio, thank your parents, and respect your teachers! Dance. *It's an awesome experience, all around, no matter where this journey takes you. My advice: it's never about your "place"—only where you take it!*

—PAM CHANCEY, CEO, PTC Productions,
The PULSE on Tour

Never ever stop educating and growing as a dancer/artist! The more rounded you are as a dancer/artist, the more you can contribute to the professional world. Most importantly, follow and dance from your heart! Listen, and take action to what you truly desire; the rest will fall into place.

—JOSEPH CORELLA, dancer, choreographer,
and Broadway performer

Regardless of your age, level of success, or creative genius, there will always be room for growth. Never let your ego stand in the way of your creative evolution!

Curtain Call

The stage went black as I ran to the quick-change booth to change costumes for the closing scene of the show. The path was familiar after five years of performing on the enormous stage, yet I noticed things I had never seen before. Everywhere I looked I saw something from a magical new perspective. Eager to take it all in, I stopped in the middle of the stage left wing and glanced out at the audience. Six thousand people sat quietly anticipating the next scene. Emotion overwhelmed me. I gazed up at the stage lights that began to fade into a beautiful color I'd managed to ignore for well over a thousand performances. I knew I would not be returning to the cast the following season, and it occurred to me how lucky I'd been to be a part of such a huge show. I began crying uncontrollably as I pulled off my costume and jumped into the next. When I entered for the final number of the show, I made eye contact with several of the other cast members who were equally shaken by their final performance. I devoured the moment as if I were the prized great white shark stealing the spotlight during Shark Week. I didn't want this feeling to end.

I ASSURE YOU, no matter how many times a show closes, wraps or comes to an end, the sentiment is always as dramatic as *The Twilight Saga: Breaking Dawn, Part 2*! We spend so much of our time in the process: the audition, the first day of rehearsal, bonding with the cast, the dress rehearsals, opening night, the fear of what we'll do once this job ends, the joy of accomplishment, the sadness when the curtain falls for the last time. We wonder, Will this be the *last* time?

> **#DanceNote**
>
> It's not enough to say you love dance if you want to be a dancer. Proclaiming your passion is a brilliant start, but you have to take action, regardless of how insignificant you think the work is.

As artists, we pour our hearts and souls into each enticing opportunity that we are fortunate to fall into. I choose the word *fall* carefully to remind you that no matter how much preparation, training, hard work, networking, and connections we have, dancers fall. Some things are out of our hands. We will not book every job. We may not like some of the jobs we book. There will be countless times when we feel like giving up.

The only advice I can give is, don't give up!

As long as you wake up engulfed with the passion and dedication that commands your soul to dance and create, then you owe it to yourself to brush yourself off, stand up tall, and try the step a different way.

There is a moment in every dancer's career when you reach a crossroad and are unsure whether you should continue performing, or (ugh) get a "real" job. Pursuing and maintaining a career in the entertainment industry requires the ability to evolve and adapt to new ideas and opportunities.

After ten years of dedicated work traveling around the world dancing, I was slowly losing my eagerness to audition and perform. (Kind of like that time you stopped taking class because you wanted to go to prom, have a boyfriend/girlfriend, or [fill in the blank].) It didn't help that the dance industry was hiring a specific type of dancer and I wasn't it. (I keep telling you, no matter who you are or how talented, everyone has downtime!)

I was bored with my daily routine of gym/Starbucks/dance class and needed a challenge. Early in my career I'd had a few chances to choreograph projects that I was also dancing in. I loved choreographing because I'm passionate about telling a story any way I can. At the time, however, I'd been too focused on my performing career to pursue it. I knew eventually there would come a time when I would further explore my voice as a choreographer. And as burnout set in after so many years touring, now seemed like the perfect moment. Without hesitation (and before I could talk myself out of it), I sent résumés to several production companies looking for choreographers. Lucky for me (and because I was willing to work for *cheap*), I scored a job choreographing for a small but important short film starring some very

On the set of *Children's Hospital* with Megan Mullally

talented actors, including Armie Hammer. The success of that short film helped me line up my next job as a choreographer. Before I knew it, I was working regularly.

Thanks to my mad skills as a social-media maven, several industry pros were aware that I was now choreo-graphing. One in particular reached out to me with an exciting opportunity. She knew a producer who was look-ing for a choreographer to work with the cast of the hit TV comedy *Children's Hospital*. Naturally, I said, *"Sign me up!"*

I spent a week working with industry legends (all of whom you will assuredly have to IMDb*) like Henry Winkler, Malin Akerman, and Megan Mullally. [Side Note: During a summer at the American Theater Dance Workshop in New York, I saw Megan Mullally perform in *How to Succeed in Business without Really Trying* on Broadway, and I've been *infatuated* ever since.] You can imagine how much fun I had on that set, choreographing for a bunch of talented and hilarious television icons! Thankfully, the producer was pleased enough with my work to recommend me for another unbelievable project. This time, I got to work with one of my comedic heroes—Ben Stiller!

Watching Ben work was invaluable to me. I marveled at his brilliance. Obviously, he knows how to be funny, but he is also so focused and committed. He will try anything, and when a joke doesn't work, he doesn't hesitate to move on. Ben possesses the exact balance of creative artistry and industry expertise needed to succeed. It is clear to me that he controls every aspect of his career but knows when to rely on the other experts with whom he collaborates.

After working with Ben, I was once again encouraged to expand my horizons. With an urgency I hadn't felt since I'd bought my first iPod, I was on the phone with my creative partner preparing for our next performing collaboration. We started writing, producing, and acting in short online parodies of our favorite reality

---

* Okay, seriously, if you don't already know about IMDb, I question your passion for entertainment. It's the world's best website. Go now! http://www.imdb.com

TV shows. Soon after our first several videos on YouTube went viral, we were flooded with awesome fan comments and critical praise. A magazine article soon followed, along with the opportunity to shoot our own TV show! (Notice how I was able to shamelessly cross-promote my work as a producer, actor, and writer, further broadening my #Brand?)

> **#DanceNote**
>
> Understanding musicality takes practice. Using the same music and choreography, explore how many ways you can interpret the dance.

You may not think of yourself as a choreographer now, but that might change once you begin working in the business. You may also decide after a few auditions or jobs that you would rather be teaching or representing dancers as an agent. I always imagined that my career as a dancer could lead to work as an actor, choreographer, director, and author. Though I wasn't sure precisely how it would happen, my willingness to say yes to unexpected opportunities naturally unlocked my artistic career. It may reinvigorate your outlook on your career as a performer, too.

You have heard enough people (myself included) tell you there is no guarantee that you will achieve success as a performer. What you need to consider is there is no guarantee that you won't either.

You have already acknowledged that you want to become a professional dancer. You made the choice to buy this book, so you must have incredibly good instincts. Don't forget to apply

On set choreographing for a Ben Stiller project

those instincts along your journey. Dare yourself to experience the scary unknown. Be fearless, and your future is limitless. The projects and adventures I value the most came from the offers I was most terrified of.

Step outside of what you think you are capable of, and unearth a career uniquely yours. Be inventive, dedicate yourself to constant growth, set new goals, and be patient: Every dancer knows timing is everything. Commit yourself to the life of an artist, and your dance will choreograph itself.

Who's Who in the Cast

DANCERS ARE brilliant artists on their own, but when you add an innovative choreographer, a magnificent story unfolds. Naming every choreographer who has left their Bloch imprint on the dance world is like trying to decide which song you *love* most in your favorite musical. Each offers a unique, expressive narrative that leaves you *#Frozen* in your seat or ready to jump up on stage and join in on the dance. While I'm positive that I've left a gaggle of talented choreographers off the list below, I share a few who have kept me in awe. I encourage you to do some #Google searching to find the choreographers who speak to you as a dancer.

Paula Abdul

You might remember her from *American Idol*, but Paula Abdul proved #OppositesAttract long before she took up flirting with Simon Cowell. Paula rocked the dance scene with her hip, grounded style of choreography and carved out a solid career

Paula Abdul
Source: Bravo/
Photofest © Bravo

as a singer and choreographer. She's no one-hit wonder, and she's got the Emmys and Grammys to prove it!

Fred Astaire

Thirty-one movie musicals spanning seventy-six years of work as a dancer, choreographer, singer, and actor make Fred Astaire my *hero*! He was the original multihyphenate and serves as my daily reminder that I can always do more.

Fred and Adele Astaire

Source: George Grantham Bain Collection, Library of Congress

George Balanchine
Source: KCBalletMedia

George Balanchine

George developed a style (and over four hundred works of choreography) so unique and his own that his legacy continues to shine with his cofounded New York City Ballet and the School of American Ballet. If you want to understand the sharp lines, dynamic attack, and beauty in the art of modern American ballet, get familiar with George Balanchine.

Mikhail Baryshnikov

Have you seen him pirouette? Beyond his ability as a dancer and choreography, I love an artist who continues to evolve. #Actor

Joshua Bergasse

Joshua made a #*Smash*-ing entrance on the prime-time scene. His work is strong and grounded yet manages to soar full of life. He's a generous teacher and choreographer, taking risks on television and stage.

Busby Berkeley

Busby Berkeley created a magical story with showgirls and sweeping camera shots. His fabulous formations were like looking through a kaleidoscope of mesmerizing colors, lines, and emotion. When you see a cool dance number in a movie today, it was likely inspired by Busby.

Zina Bethune

Zina started off at the School of American Ballet, and by age fourteen she was dancing with the New York City Ballet. Like many dancers, Zina expanded her success into an accomplished film and television career and later became a director. It was her work encouraging children with disabilities to dance with her company Infinite Dreams, however, that leaves me grateful that I had the privilege to work with her.

Andy Blankenbuehler

In class or in rehearsal, Andy is unafraid to hide his passion and love of dance. His encouraging demeanor is second only to his collaborative spirit. His choreography will have you rocking out *#InTheHeights* from *9 to 5*.

Matthew Bourne

Matthew made male swans cool! With his #Dark and #Edgy #Broadway production of *Swan Lake*, Matthew Bourne broke down gender barriers in dance and forever secured a spot center stage.

Marguerite Derricks

There are few choreographers who remember what it's like to be a dancer. Marguerite is one of them. Her choreography is always fresh and fun to watch and perform. More importantly, after working with her on *#Bunheads*, I can tell you that she is kind to her dancers and values the creative process, collaboration, and the art of storytelling.

Nacho Duato

Nacho is a genuine dancers' choreographer, which is evident in his impressive résumé, detailing his work with prestigious ballet companies around the world. The bonus is that audiences everywhere—just like the dancers who work with him—devour his mesmerizing musicality, beautiful lines, and wit.

Tabitha and Napoleon D'umo
Source: Kristin Dos Santos

Tabitha and Napoleon D'umo

I haven't had the honor to work with this dynamite Emmy-winning duo *yet*, but they're on my short list of ingenious artists to collaborate with. Their leading-edge musicality and soulful storytelling is so specific and stylized that they've branded a fierce dance-clothing line, too!

Anne Fletcher

Anne started out as a dancer and worked her way up from assisting to choreographing, and now she's directing #HollywoodBlockbusters! She cares about the artist and the art of telling a fabulous story.

Bob Fosse

#EGOT winner (Emmy, Grammy, Oscar, and Tony Awards) Bob Fosse gave us *All That Jazz* and so much more. #Sensual, #Stylized, and emotionally charged, his work continues to be replicated but *never* replaced.

Brian Friedman

Brian Friedman is #Toxic—or at least his choreography is. Friedman set the trend for a new generation of contemporary choreography that continues to #Pop on MTV.

Gus Giordano

There's a reason this legend lives on in dance textbooks. In addition to authoring the *Anthology of American Jazz Dance*, Giordano was an innovative choreographer who has often been labeled the Godfather of Jazz. But to me he will always be the mentor who hired me to perform his work and travel the world.

Gene Kelly

Gene Kelly had movie star good looks and mastered the art of the Hollywood movie musical. This Oscar-nominated entertainer made a huge splash in *Singin' in the Rain* and helped make #Ballet cool among the mainstream.

Gene Kelly in *Singin' in the Rain*, 1952
Source: MGM/Photofest © MGM

Mia Michaels

Unless you've been dedicated to endless hours in the dance studio without a TV, you're familiar with Mia Michaels's work on *So You Think You Can Dance*. After watching her work firsthand, I assure you, Mia's contemporary choreography continues to evolve like the artist herself, taking on a life full of emotion and power—always commanding a standing ovation.

Kenny Ortega

This man doesn't just *work* with legends—including the late Michael Jackson—he's a legend himself! Kenny is the man responsible for choreographing some of the most iconic movies in modern time, including *Dirty Dancing*, the movie that kick-started my career.

Travis Payne

He's worked with Lady Gaga and the King of Pop, and Travis remains one of the most generous, talented, and crafted choreographers in the business. Also a former-dancer-turned-choreographer, Travis remains true to the emotion of the piece and the performers involved.

Jerome Robbins

Tony Awards and Oscar aside, Jerome Robbins's choreography in *West Side Story* made me want to rip a pair of jeans and get into a hitch-kick fight with my rival dance studio. He's a master of the art of storytelling through choreography.

Wade Robson

Former MTV music video superstar turned *So You Think You Can Dance* Emmy-winning choreographer, Wade's signature style and clever choreography keep him an eight count ahead of the pack.

Susan Stroman

Susan made *Contact* with Broadway audiences without words. She has inspired a new generation of theatergoers to appreciate the art of storytelling through exhilarating, emotional, and electric dance.

Jerome Robbins on the set of *West Side Story*, 1961
Source: Ernst Haas, United Artists/Photofest © United Artists

Twyla Tharp

Twyla is another trailblazing choreographer. She had Broadway #*Movin'Out* of her way, with dynamic partnering work and nonstop athletic action. Twyla is always focused on breaking boundaries. It's her work as an author, however, that continues to activate my creativity and desire. Check out her books—*The Creative Habit* and *The Collaborative Habit*.

Travis Wall

After exploding onto the set of *So You Think You Can Dance* as a competitor, Travis demonstrated his natural talent and charisma as a dancer. Only after he returned to the show as a choreographer

Twyla Tharp (left), with David Byrne
Source: Sire/Photofest © Sire

did he prove that he is a force for a new generation—a story-teller to watch. Expect brilliant things from Travis Wall.

Christopher Wheeldon

If George Balanchine is the father of American ballet, Chris-topher Wheeldon is like the modern-day Prince. With over twenty works composed, his risk-taking choreography, strong point of view, and style will undoubtedly gleam #CenterStage for generations to come.

#BackstageConfessionals

I DON'T BELIEVE in #Gossip. That doesn't mean, however, there isn't room for a little backstage confessional every once in a while. As you begin your career in the entertainment industry, you will quickly discover that you never know where an adventure will find you. Having the opportunity to write a book but *not* sharing these #Fabulous tales would be as neglectful as running into [insert your favorite celebrity here] at Starbucks and *not* taking a selfie with them to brag on Instagram. Here are a few more of my favorite stories that I still can't believe really happened.

#FromShowroomToShowtime

My first week in New York City, I learned right away that while I was waiting to be discovered as the next Broadway sensation I needed to get a job. I lived on the Upper West Side, and my goal was to find a job that would be both close to home and understanding of the fact that I'd moved to the Empire State in order to be a performer, not a lifelong sales clerk. As much as I wanted the employee discount on every totally trendy and well-styled piece of clothing that J.Crew, Gap, and Banana Republic offered, I *hated* folding clothes, so I knew that working in a retail clothing store was out. I detest smelling like food all day even more than I despise celebrities who complain about too much media attention, so I knew I could never again work in a restaurant. I *loved* Starbucks far too much to make it an obligation, and, besides, each conveniently located coffeehouse was like the living room I didn't have in my shoebox apartment and the creative space where I wrote on a daily basis. Fortunately, even in my early twenties I had a flair for design and home improvements. Pottery Barn provided the perfect option to fit my need for a flexible schedule, required *no* folding, and possessed an environment that fulfilled my passion for creativity and design. After a stellar interview (in which I convinced the store manager that he should invest in a new sofa bed to accommodate an unwanted long-term houseguest), I was hired as a design-studio specialist at their most popular (albeit pricey) flagship home-decor store.

After just three weeks, I came to the affirmed realization that I could not *wait* to flee the abuse generously offered by an onslaught of self-entitled, demanding, and rage-filled customers. No offense to Pottery Barn—I still melt in their cozy, down-wrapped sofas and drool over their perfectly scented candles—I just didn't realize how ruthless retail work is. Case in point: One day an exceptionally awful Upper East Side woman screamed at me for twenty minutes because she wanted to return an accent lamp that she claimed was broken. When I assured her she simply needed to change the lightbulb, she screamed the most offensive insult she could think of, calling me "Madonna"

(I had a beauty mark on my face that I've since removed—*not* because of her) in an attempt to humiliate me in front of the other costumers.

Tragically, I am not a #TrustFund baby. So if I wanted to eat and pay rent, I had to keep the job! Rather than spend my time at work in a constant state of depression, I decided to pretend that I was on a TV show (imagine the cast of *Friends* working together at a retail store). Every cranky customer was just another guest star on the show, and my "character" could react however I saw fit. It was easy to keep this fantasy going, thanks to all of the famous people who browsed for fabulous home furnishings. Diane Keaton, Meredith Vieira, Gretchen Mol, and Dianne Wiest were all among the "series regulars" shopping for overpriced throw pillows and were far more delightful than your run-of-the-mill crabby consumers. Out of all the savvy celebrity shoppers, however, my absolute favorite was Rosie O'Donnell.

At the time, Rosie had a very popular talk show and was an outspoken advocate for live theater and the Broadway community. One afternoon, Rosie walked into the store, and I prepared to stalk her like a crazy #JustinBieber fan. I wanted to tell her how much I loved her show and that I, too, aspired to be on Broadway. *Instead* I said the only words I could muster: "Welcome to Pottery Barn; is there anything I can help you with?"

She replied, "Yes, I'd like to buy that chair."

I assured her that I would be happy to help her. When I informed her that there would be a six-week delivery time, she asked, "Why can't I just buy that chair in the store?"

After some serious begging (where I put my acting classes to great use), I managed to convince the corporate office to let me sell the floor sample to Rosie O'Donnell. She was so thrilled and grateful for my help that she invited me to personally bring the chair up to her home. Not only did I get to leave work (and get paid for it), but I got to hang out with Rosie O'Donnell in her home.

That afternoon, I recruited a stock guy to help me carry the Pottery Barn Basic Down-Wrapped Linen Twill Slipcover Chair out of the store, around Broadway and Sixty-Eighth Street, through the building's security checkpoint, and up to the thirty-third floor. To my astonishment, when I rang the doorbell we were greeted by none other than Rosie herself. She led us down a foyer that was covered in black-and-white-framed photos of the comedienne-turned-queen-of-daytime-TV-turned-Broadway-personality herself, posing with *every* famous celebrity you can think of. To say it was surreal for this struggling young dancer would be a gross understatement. After Tito (the stock guy) and I sat the chair down in her comfortably furnished and incredibly beautiful living room, she offered us each a beer and a very generous tip. Rosie was engaging. She asked me what I wanted to do with my life and what brought me to New York. I told her that I was a performer and wanted to be on Broadway. She responded, "Stick with it, stay focused, and work hard. You're definitely good looking, and you have a great personality."

That was all I needed to hear to motivate me to do even more. After that night, I took twice as many dance classes, enrolled in a new acting class, paid top dollar for the best vocal coach I could find, and went to every audition I could. Soon after, I booked my first big show in New York and sang, "So long, Pottery Barn!" This meant I had more free time to take classes at Broadway Dance Center, and I ended up working with a lot of up-and-coming choreographers. One in particular, Christopher Gattelli, was choreographing for a Broadway Cares

Me performing with Rosie O'Donnell in the Sixteenth Annual
Easter Bonnet Competition for Broadway Cares/Equity Fights AIDS.
Thank you, BC/EFA, for the important work that you do
and for allowing me to share this photo!
Source: Broadway Cares/Equity Fights AIDS

benefit, and he asked me to perform in the opening number.
Without hesitation, I said yes, and on the first day of rehearsal I
found out that Rosie O'Donnell would be performing with us. I
was #CoolWordForBeingExcited.

In less than one year's time I'd gone from lowly Pottery
Barn sales boy to actual Broadway chorus dancer, and the cool-
est part is that Rosie O'Donnell was there for both moments. I
approached her during rehearsal, and while she remembered

my face, she couldn't quite remember how she knew me. Once I filled her in, she gave me a big hug and said, "See? I knew you'd make it! . . . And I still love my chair!"

#TheGoldenGig

Like every aspiring performer, my childhood was filled with daydreams of #Fame and #Fortune. I practiced my Oscar-acceptance speech in the bathroom mirror on a daily basis while getting ready for school. Between applying hot-oil treatments and gently exfoliating away my #Acne, I visualized holding that radiant golden statue, what I would say, how it would feel. *Never* did I imagine that, one day, I might actually *become* a golden statue. Alas, when you're a young, struggling (broke) dancer trying to make it, you'd be surprised what gigs* you end up working to make ends meet.

After five weeks of six-hour rehearsal days as an unpaid apprentice in a dance company while living on instant mashed potatoes that my grandma sent me via a care package from Colorado and adding ketchup that I'd "borrowed" from McDonalds, I finally got a phone call to audition for a hair show. A well-known hair-product company was hiring dancers to perform in a trade show at the Chicago Convention Center. They were looking for "young, hot dancers willing to wear body paint." The job paid two thousand dollars and only lasted a week, so, obviously, I jumped on the "L" train and headed to the audition. Following a three-hour "improv" audition, the casting director confirmed my availability and booked me for the job right on the spot. I

---

* *Gigs* are short, independent performance opportunities that you are lucky to book between jobs. Somehow they pop up when expected and manage to pay just enough to cover the rest of your rent or grocery bills.

received my call time and was instructed to bring a robe and to "wear clothing that you don't care about." Um, did I tell you that I was broke? I cared about *every single thread of my clothing.* A new wardrobe wasn't really in my budget, as evidenced by my diet of just-add-water foods and swiped table sauce.

I arrived at the trade-show venue ready for a fun adventure. What I experienced instead was a lesson in humility. In all of my excitement about booking a job that paid so well, it had never occurred to me to ask exactly what I'd be doing. #LessonLearned. After being greeted by a slightly older and somewhat shady "hair-care expert," I was led down a hallway backstage that felt longer than the Yellow Brick Road. On either side of the corridor, gorgeous male and female models in fashion-forward designer clothes were going through hair and makeup for the big runway show. I was elated to be a part of the glamorous life! I'd never thought I would get to be a "model" because of my made-for-TV *five-foot-eight-inch* frame. And yet there I was, on the verge of making my big fashion debut.

We finally arrived at the very end of the hallway to a small "changing booth" that was really more of a see-through curtain (like they have at fancy designer clothing stores). I was handed a gold piece of thread, instructed to strip down, put the G-string on, and meet with the makeup artist who would apply the gold body paint. #ExcuseMe? That's right—I'd been hired to be a go-go dancer! I felt my heart sink into my golden thong. How on earth was I going to tell my mom—never mind the fact that I had to dance around on stage in a G-string and gold body paint alongside these tall runway divas?

By my third day, I was just so grateful to have a paycheck that I had released the embarrassment of walking past the models between shows. I figured no one had to find out about this random gig, right? If only I had been so fortunate. A photographer from the *Chicago Tribune* happened to snap a photo of my "Golden Moment," and, lucky for me, it made the front page of the Metro section. My ego hurt almost as much as my skin from the gold body paint that managed to creep its way into *every* orifice of my body. And, yes, it ruined my clothes. But at least I could finally afford solid food again!

#DancingWithTheStars

Occasionally, as dancers, we get to work with A-list celebrities, and sometimes they're even nice. Another perk of the #DanceLife is that often we get to travel to exotic locations like London, Paris, Rome, or Berlin. Other times you get stuck in (un)lucky Las Vegas. The latter was the case when I booked a gig working alongside the talented (and hilarious) Jason Alexander and the legendary vocal diva (and believe me, she lived up to the legend) Jenifer Lewis. We were singing and dancing for a televised comedy special to raise awareness about global warming. Apparently, nothing accentuates the seriousness of Al Gore's global-warming warnings like a bunch of Hollywood comedians assuring the television audience that there is still hope. That's where I entered the scene from stage left with Jason, Jenifer, and a small cast of ensemble dancers to perform a musical number for the show.

As I mentioned in chapter 6's section #WhatToExpectOn-Set, the rehearsal process is always a unique experience, and, in this case, we'd started rehearsals in Los Angeles before ever heading to Sin City. On the first day, we met Jason—friendly, engaging, and enthusiastic about performing in Vegas (which we later discovered was his masked exuberance about playing poker all night long)—and Jenifer—loud, opinionated, and absolutely hilarious. After formal introductions, we learned our music and choreography, ran the number a few times, and swapped nerdy musical-theater stories. Some of the best #BackstageConfessionals come from the actual celebrity insiders willing to spill the juicy details!

The week of the show, we flew to Las Vegas and were put up in our own suite at the fabulous Caesars Palace. My room (which was roughly three times the size of my first studio apartment in New York City) had its own hot tub, wine bar, and flat-screen TV (long before Best Buy was giving them away as door prizes). I felt like a member of the Rat Pack.* Once we were settled into our rooms, we were sent to our costume fittings, rehearsals, sound check, and finally our final run-through for camera blocking. During the camera blocking, I had my first encounter with a #Celeb on the star-studded stage. Faith Hill was finishing up her sound check, and as we were walking onto the stage, she was gliding off. Not only was she stunningly beautiful, but she took a moment to say hello to each and every one of the dancers and to support her fellow performers. She even praised the timeless comedic stylings of a certain stand-up-comedian-turned-movie-star, who in turn responded like a total #Jerk. My eyes darted away from the situation like an airline passenger unwilling to make eye contact with you because they know they're in your aisle seat and don't want to give it up. #NotAllCelebritiesAreNice

After finishing the dress rehearsal, we were released into the gambling capital of the world with a thick wad of per diem† and told to meet the following morning in a random hotel ballroom for a run-through before the show. I went to dinner with

---

* Please Google that reference!

† A *per diem* is an additional amount of money that you are given to cover costs of food and travel expenses for each day you are working out of town.

some of the dancers from my cast, spent *all* of my per diem on clothes from the Forum Shops at Caesars, and went back to my lavish hotel room for a relaxing spa evening to guarantee a camera-ready me for the day of the show.

The next morning, after a breakfast comprising graciously comped goodies from the hotel minibar, and obviously no alcohol, I made my way down to rehearsal. Jenifer Lewis was prompt and eager to begin, because she had to "get to hair and makeup" as soon as possible. Jason, who is very professional and easy to work with, showed up, let's just say, a *little* late. Apparently his per diem was bankrolling an *investment* at the poker table, on which he was still awaiting an actual return. Following a successful brush-up rehearsal, we made our way to the dressing rooms and then backstage. The minute I stepped onto the stage at Caesars Palace (the very same stage that Celine Dion, Cher, Elton John, and many more had performed on), my nerves kicked in to full grumble mode. I wasn't expecting to get so excited and freak out—it's not like this was my first time performing. I'd never really experienced nerves like this, but I chalked it up to the combination of Snickers, Peanut M&Ms, and salt-and-vinegar potato chips I'd eaten for breakfast. Before I knew it, our intro music played. Jason was as cool as a cucumber. (He probably enjoyed a fancy steak-and-egg breakfast.) He came up to me and said, "Are you going to the cast party afterward?"

"The what?" I said while trying to hold down a mouthful of "nerves."

"There's a cast party afterward. I hope you guys are going to be there."

"Oh, well, I don't think we were invited," I mumbled.

"Consider this an invitation. You're a part of the cast, and you should be there. If anyone asks, tell them I invited you."

Greenroom snapshot with Jason Alexander and
ensemble . . . minus the champagne!

"Thanks, Jason! Okay, I'm going to go on stage now."

"See you out there!"

And like that, I was on stage in full autopilot. Soon, our
Mother Nature–loving song and dance was near the end, and
so were the butterflies flying around my stomach. I savored the
opportunity to ham it up for a big finish (jazz hands included)
with Jason Alexander.

After #NameDropping the invitation from Jason Alexander,
we got to hang backstage in the greenroom amid flawless eco-
friendly decor, an environmentally conscious gourmet spread,
and the finest bubbly. Oh, and did I mention that in addition to
Jason, Jenifer, and Faith I was rubbing elbows with Tom Hanks,
Bill Maher, Tim McGraw, Wanda Sykes, Julia Louis-Dreyfus,
Larry David, and Leonardo DiCaprio? I'm a fearlessly outgoing
person, always ready to make the most of an opportunity, so I

decided to engage in conversation with as many of the A-listers as possible. Who cares if these people had more Oscars and Grammys combined than I had dollars in my bank account? I couldn't get fired from the job, because I'd already performed. The worst they could do was kick me out of the greenroom. To my delight, nearly all of them were extremely engaging and #Awesome. And, note, the food and expensive champagne were marvelous, too.

The show was coming to an end, and the incredibly hilarious Wanda Sykes was on stage performing her set. I stood in between Julia Louis-Dreyfus and Leo—otherwise known as Leonardo DiCaprio (but in my mind we were already totally on a first-name basis). Wanda finished the punch line to her last joke, and, as with all of her material, it was PYPF! (That's *pee-your-pants funny*, for those of you who aren't down with the lingo.) Leo turned to me laughing out loud, looked me right in the eyes, put his hands on my shoulders, and said, "That was great!"

Time stood still. I felt like such an *insider*. Agreed, the joke was great, but the fact that Leonardo DiCaprio actually touched me was insane. Convinced that some of his A-list magic might rub off on me, I decided it was probably for the best that I preserve the shirt I was wearing and touch it whenever I had an audition. The five-time Academy Award nominee and I shared a moment of laughter backstage at a show we'd both been in, and that's the beauty of being a performer.

As a dancer, you might not be a recognizable celebrity, but you're still a part of an insider's club—a group of crazy, funny, emotional, and creative artists who share brilliant moments together. The after-party was off the hook, but, come on, nothing can really compare to the backstage camaraderie! Oh, and I *still* haven't washed that shirt.

#Cut!

Picture an overcrowded holding room full of LA's best-looking, most-talented working dancers, including every industry friend you've *ever* worked with, and the entire cast from each season of *So You Think You Can Dance*. One by one, we handed over our picture, résumé, and signed release form allowing cameras, strategically placed in every direction you looked, to capture the entire audition process. Think of it like *The Real World: #Dance Edition*. My point is, there was no place you could go where you weren't being filmed. It was the first time I understood how a Kardashian might feel shopping for toilet paper (we all do it, but not on camera). It's already a challenge to learn a piece of choreography at an audition, but add cameras, the industry's hottest dancers, and Mia Michaels, and the pressure is on!

Having already worked with Mia Michaels several years earlier while I'd been dancing with Giordano Dance Chicago, I was prepared for a long audition process with a very demanding, opinionated, and short-tempered perfectionist. To my delight and surprise, Mia entered the room and could not have been more gracious, humble, or excited to be working with all of the eager hopefuls (myself included).

The audition started off like most do. Mia, who was also an executive producer and lead on the project, gave a very inspiring speech. She thanked us for taking the time to audition for her new show. Moreover, she expressed sincere gratitude for allowing the production crew to film us and use the footage however they saw fit. (This is an important factor to the story, one that I hadn't really considered or concerned myself with at the time.)

We began learning the combination, which started off subtle. It was a very grounded modern-jazz phrase, with strong accents, cool transitions, and nice acting moments. Mia mentioned (while her assistant demonstrated the choreography) that they were looking for a wide variety of dancers who were strong actors, and she assured us to not get discouraged. I was relieved and felt like I actually had a great chance of booking this job. After running the first six counts of eight a few times through, switching lines and listening to feedback, I thought we were going to begin the next phase of the audition process. How wrong I was! It turns out we'd only learned one-third of the dance. My heart sank as I realized this was going to be one of "those" auditions—the kind that lasts all day and requires every ounce of technique, willpower, and false confidence. Sure enough, Mia's assistant continued with the next phrase of choreography, which incorporated slow developpés and sustained leg tilts. Oh, goody—my favorite! #Sarcasm. Every new count of eight set in motion fast-paced direction changes, pirouette combinations, and outrageous jumps from low lunge to soaring switch arabesques. Television and film choreography rarely involves such intricate, technical elements. What happened to step touch, step touch, kick ball change, step pose? Mia's fearless choreography would have been a dream if we'd had more than two hours to perfect every twist, tilt, and turn.

I considered sneaking out of the room, but my ego demanded that I stay. I did not want to be one of "those" dancers who discretely exits the audition, leaving behind only their headshot, résumé, and pride when their name is called *out loud* enough times for everyone in the room to realize they'd given up. I went to the back of the room, which was engulfed in the smell of sweat and desperation, to review the choreography, where I was relieved to find a dozen other dancers who were also tormented by their former ability and the struggle to "get through this audition." I worked carefully on learning where I could really hold back and use my acting skills. So what if my leg doesn't extend like the graceful limbs of a prima ballerina in her prime? I'm a guy. It never did. And, besides, I'm giving major intensity with my #Face! The clock was ticking, and it was nearly time to start breaking off into groups for the first cut. I went to my dance bag to towel off, gather my thoughts, and digest about fifteen Advil Liqui-Gels. I was in the third group of dancers to get called, which I was totally comfortable with. Usually, I like to be in the first group to get it over with, but auditioning with a later group gave me the chance to relax and trust that my training and years of experience would not betray me. I watched the first set of dancers perform, and they were young, flexible, and fabulous! During the second group, I closed my eyes and ran the dance in my head with the music: "If I can visualize it, I can nail it!" Suddenly, it was my turn. There were five people total in my group. Surrounded by an army of exhausted dancers looking on and a legion of cameramen, we walked out to the dance floor and took our spots in front of a panel of producers, creative executives, and casting directors. I felt like a criminal facing a firing squad: "You have been convicted of aspiring to dance on a TV show where the average contestant is half your age. Do you have any last words?"

The music started, and my subconscious began delivering an inner pep talk to my ego while I maneuvered through each section of the choreography. "*Yes.* You're doing it," I thought, as I continued to gain confidence and slowly started to savor the delicious layers in the choreography. With each isolation, contraction, and battement, I was growing more courageous and invested in my performance. Then, it happened. I was transitioning from a deep lunge on my left leg, ready to change directions with the chaîné coupe jeté toward stage right. As I was midway through the shift, I launched full-forced toward the rest of my group of dancers, who were currently midair in the jeté headed straight toward me. Like a bug meeting its death on the windshield of a car traveling sixty-five miles an hour down the freeway, I struck one of the guys in my group while soaring through the air. #MatrixStyle, we collided and dropped to the floor. He tripped over my wrecked body and continued with the dance as I sluggishly peeled myself off the floor and hit my final pose.

Unable to distinguish the pain in my entire body from the black-and-blue bruises to my pride, I stood there while the panel of creative killers talked among themselves, barely able to hold back the laughter. Minus the sound of ten digital cameras capturing every mortifying moment, the room stood in silence for the first time all day. Mia asked me what happened, and all I could say was, "I guess I just felt like exploring a different direction." With that, the room burst into laughter, and I was cut.

I'd never been more excited to get out of an audition room! I dodged all of my friends who were making their way toward me to offer kind but totally useless words of encouragement (I didn't need to hear, "It wasn't as bad as you think"). I was there, okay? I know exactly how awful it was! I got in my car and called my agent, recapping every gruesome detail. We shared a solid laugh, until I remembered . . . the cameras! OMG! What were they going to do with that footage? I'd look like an idiot. She assured me that it would be okay. And, after a few months of embarrassment every time I went to an audition, it was.

Eventually people forget, and you book another job, and you're back on top. We all have our less-than-flattering moments in this industry. Mine just happened to be caught on camera. The TV show never aired, but I know the footage exists, most likely floating around in a digital space waiting for the perfect occasion to land and punish me once again. I imagine that one day I'll be receiving some huge honor, and, while I'm giving my acceptance speech (the one that I practiced daily with silky hair and bad skin), they'll play the clip as a reminder that you should never take yourself too seriously in life or in art.

Encore!

D
ANCERS CAN move a set piece, change costumes, safety pin a broken shoe strap, reapply false eyelashes, solve a BFF's relationship problems, and make dinner reservations at the trendiest hotspot, all within a thirty-second quick-change. So, how do you catapult all of that ingenuity and years of training into a successful career?

Lucky for you, I've stockpiled my years of nerd-level notes precisely for a moment like this. While I encourage you to take advantage of the information I supply, I also urge you to take the initiative to continue expanding your knowledge of dance wherever you can. Read *Dance Spirit* and *Dance Magazine*. Get to know the power players in the world of dance by seeing every live event in your city (most venues provide student pricing and discounted shows). Go online and learn about your field, or go to a library to study the history of dance. Collaborate with as many choreographers and dancers as you can, and make sure to take notes along the way!

Dance Magazine, http://www.dancemagazine.com/

#BestOnlineResource

I'm elated that you bought my book! Seriously, I know that bookstores are harder to find than a zit on Kristen Stewart's snow-white complexion. Nevertheless, it's the twenty-first century, and you practically grew up with an iSomething attached to your palm from birth, so please take advantage of the Internet. Answers4dancers is by far the most up-to-date resource for dancers and choreographers. In addition to posting information for worldwide auditions, teaching positions, and advice, Answers4Dancers provides sample résumés, headshot dos and don'ts, industry updates, interviews with top choreographers and dancers, tips on how to get an agent, and so much more.

Answers4Dancers, http://www.answers4dancers.com/

#FindingAnAgent

Once you have settled into your new city, it may be time to start meeting with agents. Finding the right agent is like shopping for the perfect pair of jeans: you might have to try on a few different sizes from several different shops before you find the smartest fit for your vibe. Likewise, you may have to meet with several agencies before you find a mutually beneficial match.

Before you reach out to a prospective agent, visit their website. Take a look at the agency's team and the clients they represent. (It's like online shopping for your career!) See if you recognize any names or faces. Make a list of questions that you have for the agent before you take your meeting. Questions might include, How many clients do you represent? Do you have clients that are similar to me, and, if so, is it a conflict of interests? It's also essential that you share with the prospective agent your long-term and short-term goals.

Pop Quiz: Remember all the tools you've been developing in acting and vocal classes, videos you've posted to YouTube, and workshops you've rocked? This is where they come in handy. Tell the agent what you hope to accomplish professionally, including any aspirations of one day transitioning into an actress, writer, comedian, or choreographer. The more versatile you are, the more they have to work with.

> **#DanceNote**
>
> To improve your flexibility, try stretching while watching TV, reading a book, or working on a project.

The target is to find an agent who understands you and where you belong in the dance industry. The relationship that you build with your agent will be much more important than the cute guy you are flirting with on Facebook, so make sure your main focus is on your career. As I mentioned in chapter 7, an agent can only work as hard for you as you work for yourself!

Once you sign with your #DreamTeam, follow their lead. Do what they tell you to do as quickly as possible. Mom and Dad aren't around anymore, so until you can afford a personal assistant, it's up to you to take care of business. Your top priority is supplying your agent with the things they need as soon as they ask for them. When they ask for more headshots, get them more headshots—not tomorrow or after you hang out with the hot new girl from class. *Now.* This industry doesn't wait around for anyone. Stay on top of your e-mails, and respond to people within one business day (sooner if possible). I have booked so many jobs just by replying yes before anyone else. Things happen quickly in the entertainment industry. I can't even count the number of dancers I know who have missed out on jobs because they do not make themselves constantly available. Don't forget about the power of social media. Market yourself on Facebook, Instagram, Twitter, and your website. When people reach out, respond!

Keep your résumé and headshot updated and fresh. Listen to the feedback choreographers and casting directors give you, and, if necessary, change up your image! If you aren't auditioning as much as you'd like, take a proactive approach by asking your representation what else you can do. Complaining to other dancers is a bad idea; you *know* gossip travels faster in the dance world than Ann Miller's nerve tap.* There's no need to act like a forgotten cast member from *90210*. If you are unhappy with your progress, take respectful action.

Below is a short list of agencies I have compiled that have proven to be long-standing industry leaders in the fields of dance and choreography. I have established relationships with dancers, choreographers, and agents at most of the agencies mentioned and can attest to their level of excellence. Don't panic if an agency you are considering isn't on this list. There are hundreds of agencies in the entertainment industry that represent dancers and choreographers. Instead of searching for the "biggest" agent, find the agency that represents you and your #Brand of dance. Most of the websites have specific information on their submission and audition processes for new clients. It's always a smart idea to compose a fun, professional, and direct cover letter to send along with your picture and résumé.

---

* Quickly YouTube *Ann Miller* and see what you've been missing.

Dance Representation

Bloc http://www.blocagency.com/
Clear Talent Group (CTG) http://cleartalentgroup.com/
Cunningham, Escott, Slevin, Doherty Talent Agency (CESD)
    http://www.cesdtalent.com/
DDO Artists Agency http://ddoagency.com/
Go 2 Talent Agency (GTA) http://www.gototalentagency.com/
McDonald Selznick Associates (MSA)
    http://www.msaagency.com/
The Movement Talent Agency
    http://www.movement-agency.com/

#UniversitiesAndConservatories

Deciding where you want to attend school is as personal as the notes you passed to your bestie during biology class—and a lot more important! Find a program that suits your needs as a dancer. Are you looking for a strong ballet department, or do you prefer jazz, musical theater, or modern? Do you plan on starting your dance career in the city where you attend college? What percentage of the prospective school's alumni continue on with a professional career? During the course of my career I've gathered a list of schools that I hear about repeatedly among colleagues and industry professionals. While these schools strive for excellence in dance and academia, and continue to develop successful working dancers, this list represents only a snippet of the exceptional dance programs across the country. I implore you to take the time to find the school that's right for you!

Dance Schools, Universities, and Conservatories

Ailey/Fordham BFA Program http://www.theaileyschool.edu/BFA
California Institute of the Arts http://calarts.edu/
Juilliard http://www.juilliard.edu/
Marymount Manhattan College http://www.mmm.edu/
New York University, Tisch School of the Arts
    http://www.tisch.nyu.edu/page/home.html
Northwestern University http://www.northwestern.edu/
Oklahoma City University http://www.okcu.edu/
Pace University http://www.pace.edu/
Point Park University http://www.pointpark.edu/
Southern Methodist University http://www.smu.edu/
State University of New York, Purchase College
    http://www.purchase.edu/
The University of Arizona http://www.arizona.edu/
University of California—Irvine http://uci.edu/
University of Nevada—Las Vegas http://www.unlv.edu/
University of North Carolina School of the Arts
    http://www.uncsa.edu/
The University of the Arts http://www.uarts.edu/

#ConcertDance

If you are a concert-dance aficionado (that's a fancy word for *fan*), chances are you have already seen a company that caught your eye. Nevertheless, I'd like to share some of the concert-dance companies I admire. Most of the ones I mention here have scholarship and apprenticeship programs where you can continue your training, build on your style, and learn company repertoire alongside the principal dancers. Check out their websites for audition and performance details.

Listing every concert-dance company across the United States is almost as impossible as watching an episode of *So You Think You Can Dance* without disagreeing with one of the judges. Whether you are a die-hard bunhead or a dynamic contemporary-jazz #Diva, I have tried to offer something for everyone. Don't forget to check out YouTube and Google for hundreds more companies that continue to create groundbreaking work.

> **#DanceNote**
>
> If you're not taking ballet, you're not living up to your full potential as a dancer. It's that simple.

Ballet Companies

American Ballet Theatre http://www.abt.org/
Boston Ballet http://www.bostonballet.org/
Houston Ballet http://www.houstonballet.org/
New York City Ballet http://www.nycballet.com/
Pacific Northwest Ballet http://www.pnb.org/
San Francisco Ballet http://www.sfballet.org/

Jazz/Contemporary Companies

Giordano Dance Chicago http://www.giordanodance.org/
Hubbard Street Dance Chicago
    http://www.hubbardstreetdance.com/
River North Dance Chicago http://rivernorthchicago.com/

Modern Companies

Alvin Ailey American Dance Theater http://www.alvinailey.org/
José Limón Dance Foundation http://limon.org/
Mark Morris Dance Group http://markmorrisdancegroup.org/
Parsons Dance http://www.parsonsdance.org/
Paul Taylor Dance Company http://ptdc.org/
Pilobolus http://www.pilobolus.com/home.jsp

#AdditionalOpportunities

There are plenty of cruise lines seeking dancers, but if you want to hit the high seas in style, see the world, and build performance experience, consider the possibilities that Royal Caribbean International provides! In addition to their own state-of-the-art production facility, you'll enjoy learning a variety of shows including Broadway favorites *Hairspray*, *Chicago*, and *Saturday Night Fever*. While I never actually performed on a cruise ship, I did have the privilege of working with a cast as a rehearsal director—all thanks to the fact that earlier in my career I'd danced in a concert-dance company in Chicago with the choreographer who went on to create many of the shows at Royal Caribbean. #Connections.

Royal Caribbean Productions

http://www.royalcaribbeanproductions.com/

Each year millions of people enjoy the festive grandeur and majesty of the Radio City Christmas Spectacular, starring the world-famous Rockettes. It happens to be the number-one-grossing show in the world; it also employs an epic cast of dancers (and live animals! #NotJoking). If you are ready to show off your eye-high kicks, look no further than Radio City Music Hall. Of note, they hire a male ensemble, too! In fact, I spent five seasons dancing and singing on the Great Stage! Once you have spent your holiday performing for millions of people from around the world, I assure you there is no cooler club. (I refer to it as a *club* because the performers I met during my time at Radio City remain my closest friends and collaborators.)

Radio City Music Hall
> http://www.radiocity.com/

Hundreds of dancers and musical-theater performers start their careers with the Walt Disney Company. Between the Mouse House's theme parks, cruise ships, and specialty shows across the globe, Mickey is *always* searching for dancers. With a wide variety of part- and full-time opportunities, union contracts, health insurance, and other benefits, Disney offers career longevity. I've had the privilege of performing in several live theatrical events and TV shows for Disney in Chicago, New York, and Los Angeles. Working for Mickey Mouse is always magical!

Disney Auditions http://www.disneyauditions.com/

#UnionWebsites

Performers' trade unions are like a secret club for professional artists. They offer resources, provide pension and health options, negotiate fair wages, fight for safe working conditions, and uphold trade integrity, and you get to carry a fancy membership card in your wallet!

Actors' Equity Association (AEA) http://www.actorsequity.org/
American Guild of Musical Artists (AGMA)
  http://www.musicalartists.org/
American Guild of Variety Artists (AGVA)
  http://www.agvausa.com/
Screen Actors Guild—American Federation of
  Television and Radio Artists (SAG-AFTRA),
  http://www.sagaftra.org/

#HelpfulHintsForYour
FirstProfessionalJob

You've booked the job! Now what? The night before your first professional gig or rehearsal can be as nerve racking as showing up in your underwear on your first day of high school.

Like the Boy Scout's motto, you should "be prepared!" Pack your dance bag like you are going on a ten-week vacation to Antarctica. Include several kinds of shoes, a pair of kneepads, a towel, deodorant, and a change of clothes to stay fresh throughout the hours of rehearsal. Fight off hunger pangs with healthy snacks like nuts, protein bars, and fruit. Don't forget water, too! Overachievers might carry a notebook and pencil to write down any choreography and blocking notes for later reference. I also encourage you to bring a book (especially while working on a TV or film set), as you may find yourself in a holding room without an Internet connection and with more downtime than a former 1980s sitcom star.

The first day on any new job is usually spent filling out mounds of paperwork, so bring your passport, social security card, or other ID for release forms and W-2s.

In the entertainment biz, first impressions are everything. Show up to rehearsal looking fresh. If you are going to a shoot, ladies, arrive without makeup or product in your hair; guys should be clean shaven (unless you have been instructed otherwise) so that the hair and makeup department will have a "clean canvas."

Just like kindergarten all over again, check in with the correct contact person, be it the choreographer, company director, rehearsal director, production assistant, or assistant director (often the first or second AD on a television set). Make friends, *not* enemies. It takes a team of people to keep any production up and running, and everyone is equally important. Try your best to remember people's names and job titles (that pad and pencil will come in handy here, too). If you plan on working in this industry for a while, there's a strong chance you will work with these people again.

Which leads me to a #Lecture: Keep your attitude positive. Negative energy spreads like wildfire on a set. No one wants to spend long days with a cranky, crabby complainer! If you encounter a serious issue that needs to be addressed, find your union representative or production manager, and explain the situation. Trust the chain of command, and enjoy a happy, creative work environment.

Along with everything I just said, I want to remind you how *brilliant* you are. Although I may not have met you personally or seen you dance (yet), I'm confident that there is a place for each of us to share our unique artistic perspective. Remember this throughout your career as a dancer. There will be smashing victories on your journey, and, no matter how successful you are or how many credits you have on your résumé, there will be periods when you won't book work. Everyone has dry spells in their career. The most challenging part of your job as a dancer is to work through those downtimes and stay positive and focused on your goals. Dancers who continue to #Werk are the dancers who continue to *work* through the dark times. It helps if you stay creative. When you aren't booking gigs, get together with friends to post videos on YouTube or to choreograph a showcase, inviting agents and casting directors to come. Do whatever it takes to stay positive, creative, and healthy so that when you get your next big break you'll be ready. If you are awesome enough to book a job once, you'll be awesome enough to book a job again.

#WERKbook
and
Creative Journal

GOOD NEWS ... this is *not* a #Test! If you've made it this far, then you've read *my* stories and heard *my* advice, so now consider this to be the perfect opportunity to explore *your* motivating passion and absorb these practical tools in a way that directly benefits your goals and objectives.

Just like do-re-mi, let's start at the very beginning with a habitual task geared toward expanding your professional career, capitalizing on your unique voice, and committing to your creative purpose. Incorporating daily check-ins will help you build a strong foundation that will keep you focused and positive. Living and working as an artist can be rough; however, if you dedicate a small amount of time daily to writing in a journal, setting goals, and seeking inspiration, you will find the process more manageable and the results more tangible.

Whether you are on the first eight count of your professional path or your adventure is well underfoot, taking your next first step is always the hardest. Fear not—I've gathered a series of exercises, tasks, and questions that will help you on the road to plotting your creative map. Encourage yourself to set aside twenty minutes a day for your #CreativeDailyCheckIn, and I promise you, you'll develop a habit that is harder to break than your addiction to #Starbucks!

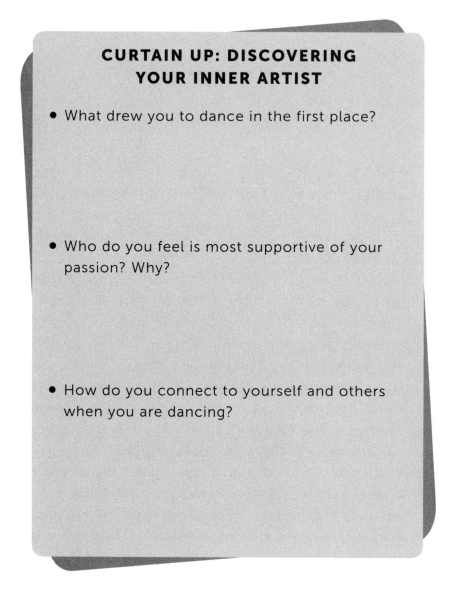

CURTAIN UP: DISCOVERING YOUR INNER ARTIST

- What drew you to dance in the first place?

- Who do you feel is most supportive of your passion? Why?

- How do you connect to yourself and others when you are dancing?

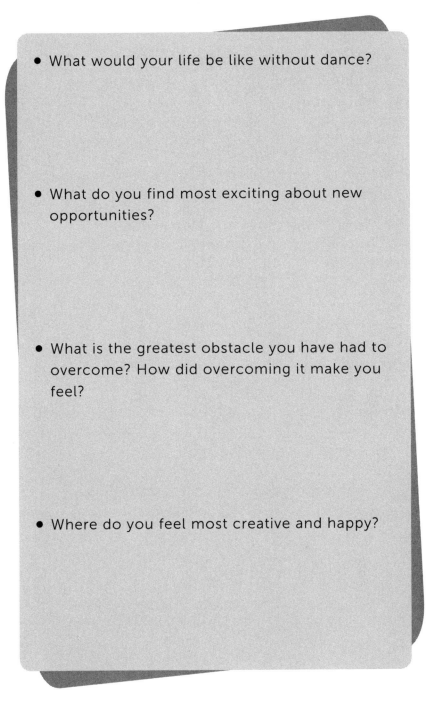

- What would your life be like without dance?

- What do you find most exciting about new opportunities?

- What is the greatest obstacle you have had to overcome? How did overcoming it make you feel?

- Where do you feel most creative and happy?

- When you're having a bad day, what makes you feel better? How does dance make you feel better?

- What is your most outrageous dream?

- Does it scare you to think about accomplishing your dream? If so, why?

- What is the greatest obstacle that stands between you and your dream?

- Do you set goals for yourself? If yes, do you find that setting goals has helped you? If no, is there a specific reason that keeps you from setting goals?

- TEN-YEAR PLAN: Identify where you would like to be in ten years. Dreams and goals often change and evolve over time, so allow yourself to visualize the big picture, staying flexible to adjusting your plan as unexpected opportunities arise.

  ○ Make a list of obstacles that stand in between you and your ten-year plan.

○ Make a list of actions you can take to break through those obstacles.

Example: My ten-year goal is to perform on Broadway, so I will set target goals over the next five years to accomplish this goal.

• FIVE-YEAR PLAN: Identify five *long-term goals* that you would like to accomplish in the next five years. These goals are slightly more out of reach at this point in your life but give you something to focus on over the next five years.

TIP

Objectives are specific *things* you dream of attaining (like conquering your center splits), while *actions* are specific *tasks* you perform to reach those objectives (if I straddle wall stretch for the duration of two slow songs a day, I can reach my objective).

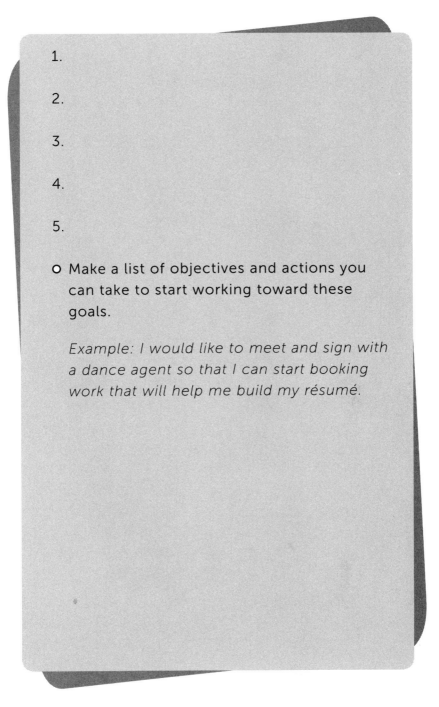

1.

2.

3.

4.

5.

O Make a list of objectives and actions you can take to start working toward these goals.

   Example: I would like to meet and sign with a dance agent so that I can start booking work that will help me build my résumé.

- THREE-YEAR PLAN: Identify where you would like to be in three years. This is the perfect time to check in and take an inventory. Make sure you're honest with yourself. Don't hide from the truth; it won't help you reach your target.

  o Are you still on track with your short-term and long-term goals?

  o Have your long-term goals changed? If so, how do you feel about those changes?

○ Do you find yourself struggling to stay on track with your short-term goals?

○ Do you feel as if you are too ambitious with your goals? If so, is this overreach affecting your ability to stay focused and positive?

• ONE-YEAR PLAN: Identify five *short-term goals* that you would like to accomplish in the next year. These should be things that are going to challenge you to push yourself but are realistically within your reach.

1.

2.

3.

4.

5.

○ Make a list of objectives and actions you can take in order to achieve these goals.

Example: I would like to have a solid résumé and dance reel and start submitting myself to dance agents.

• SIX-MONTH PLAN: Identify where you would like to be in six months. This is a fun way to develop the habit of setting goals and to experience the joy of accomplishment. Make sure to set goals that are well within your reach. You should be able to actively work at these goals every day.

Example: I would like to commit to creative writing every day for fifteen minutes.

Example: I would like to learn a new style of dance.

Example: I would like to take an acting class to improve on my emotional connection to dance.

Example: I would like to record myself dancing and put together a reel of my work.

- ONE-MONTH PLAN: Identify where you would like to be in one month.

  ○ Tell yourself, My dream is to perform in a Broadway show, so I will:

    Example: Spend ten minutes a day working on learning a new song to sing at auditions.

    Example: Work on a scene or monologue in order to grow as a performer.

    Example: Double the number of ballet classes I take this month in order to strengthen my technique.

- DAILY GOALS: What do you want to achieve on a daily basis? These goals will change often.

  Example: I will work on my center splits in order to gain flexibility.

  Example: I will go online every day and watch a new dance video to expand my knowledge of dance.

  Example: I will #Google Broadway shows in order to discover the shows that I might audition for someday.

  Example: I will be more positive when receiving feedback in class. I will keep track of my corrections and improve on my ability to apply them in class.

- Do your *short-term goals* align with your *long-term goals*? Go back and make adjustments as necessary. How does each of these lists affect where you imagine yourself in ten years?

TIP: As you accomplish your short-term goals, how do they affect your long-term goals? Are you reaching things faster? Do you need more time? Should you set new challenges?

Right to the Pointe: Work Smarter in Class

. . . especially while incorporating your daily goals and journaling . . .

- My favorite style of dance is:

- My least-favorite style of dance is:

- I'm most inspired to dance when:

- I get frustrated in class when:

- I get excited in class when:

- The thing I love most about dancing is:

- Five things that limit me as a dancer are:

  Example: My jumps and pirouettes.

  Example: Musical interpretation.

  Example: My lack of flexibility.

  1.

  2.

  3.

  4.

  5.

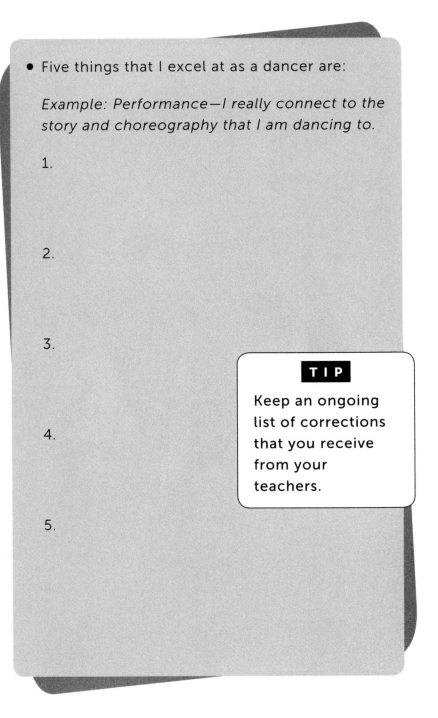

- Five things that I excel at as a dancer are:

Example: Performance—I really connect to the story and choreography that I am dancing to.

1.

2.

3.

4.

5.

TIP

Keep an ongoing list of corrections that you receive from your teachers.

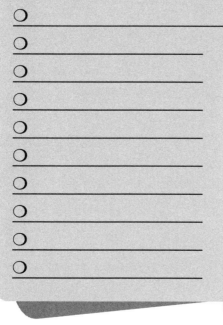

#ClassNotes

Choreography Notes and Ideas

Understanding who you are as a dancer is critical to your transformation from dedicated student to working professional. Articulating your strengths and weaknesses, goals and setbacks will accelerate your learning process and make it that much easier to leap from the training studio to the rehearsal hall. Developing the habit of taking notes in a class environment will come in handy when you're working a professional job. In a professional setting, the director or choreographer will hold a "note session" after each rehearsal, and if you don't apply the notes they give, you may find yourself unemployed!

○ _____

○ _____

○ _____

○ _____

○ _____

○ _____

○ _____

○ _____

○ _____

○ _____

TIP

Write the corrections and notes you receive *immediately* after class, review the list at the beginning of each class, and work to implement the changes.

Inspiration

As dancers, it is important that we evolve artistically and challenge our intellects in order to create new work. Set aside two hours each week to seek inspiration outside of the dance studio. Suggested activities follow.

- Visit a museum, find a painting or sculpture that speaks to you, and write the story that you think is being told. Doing this will help you connect with your own personal stories that you will later apply to the emotional aspects of your performing career.

- What genre of music do you hear while you are writing the tale?

- What style of dance do you imagine choreographing in order to complement your story?

- Grab your smartphone, if you have one, strike your best selfie pose that you feel represents the story of the artwork you described, and post it to Instagram *right now*—hashtags #DanceNotes #IWasCreativeToday! @FunnyShaffer

- Watch a documentary on a style of dance or choreographer that you are unfamiliar with.

- Record a fifteen-second video of your best interpretation of the choreography you watched, and post it to Instagram right now—hashtags #DanceNotes #NameOfChoreographer. @FunnyShaffer

- Take a walk through the park or along the beach and with your smartphone capture a video of surrounding nature, animals, and people interacting. Does this spark an idea?

- Study these videos, and use them to experiment with new moves that you can incorporate into your current dance style and voice.

TIP

Make sure to tag @funnyshaffer and watch for my special online promotions, reposts of your videos and pictures, and inspirations from what others just like you are posting!

- Google search a new city, using the words *dance*, *dancers*, *dance companies*, and *performing arts*, and get familiar with new concert-dance companies, choreographers, and dancers each week via YouTube.

- My favorite ballet company is _____, and what speaks to me about their style of movement is:

- My favorite modern company is
  _____, and what is different
  and/or similar about them from the kind
  of movement I have learned is:

- My favorite jazz company is _____,
  and I find them to be a relevant contributor to
  the world of dance today because:

- Dancers who rock my world, and why they
  move me, are:

- Choreographers who get me all warm and fuzzy inside, and the reasons I'm so in love with their work, are:

- This Broadway musical is the bomb: _____ . It inspires me to:

- I'm in #Love with this dance movie: _____ . When I watch it I:

Creative Notes

"God, I Hope I Get It": #Auditions

Dancers book approximately one in every one hundred jobs for which they audition. Those odds can feel overwhelming; however, if you keep track of your progress and take notes of your growth, you have a greater chance at beating those odds faster than Paloma Herrera's petit allegro and at booking with greater frequency and consistency.

- The following are choreographers with whom I have a great working relationship:

- The following are choreographers with whom I want to work:

- The following are five things I can do to gain the opportunity to work with them:

  Example: Find a master class or workshop that they are teaching.

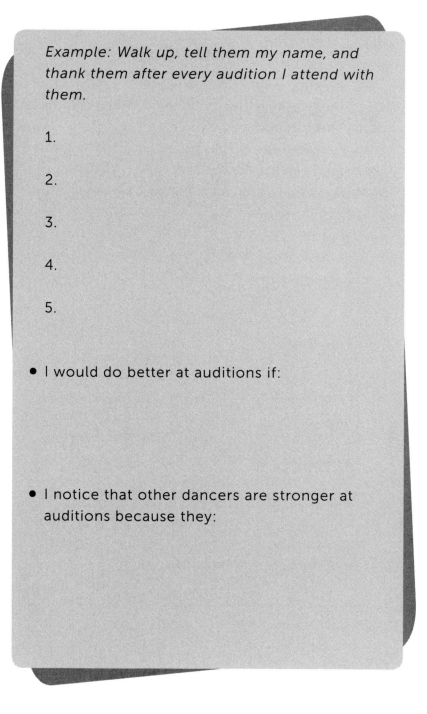

Example: Walk up, tell them my name, and thank them after every audition I attend with them.

1.

2.

3.

4.

5.

- I would do better at auditions if:

- I notice that other dancers are stronger at auditions because they:

- Do I pick up choreography easily at auditions? If no, the following are five things I can do to improve on this:

Example: Regularly try new classes to build the skills of learning styles of choreography that are unfamiliar to me.

Example: Attend master classes with different teachers.

Example: Drop in on new classes, just to change up my style. (It's fun to nail it every time, but if you don't risk failure, you'll never stand a chance at true success!)

1.

2.

3.

4.

5.

- If I had to choose my favorite style of dance, it would always be _____, because it makes me feel:

- If I had to choose my least-favorite style of dance, it would be _____, because it makes me feel:

- In order to increase my opportunity to work, I would enjoy the above style of dance more if I were to: (#Remember, the more you can do, the more you #Werk!)

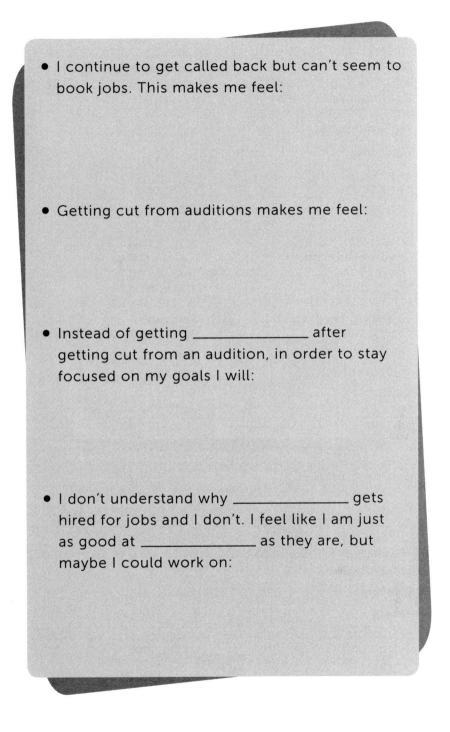

- I continue to get called back but can't seem to book jobs. This makes me feel:

- Getting cut from auditions makes me feel:

- Instead of getting _____ after getting cut from an audition, in order to stay focused on my goals I will:

- I don't understand why _____ gets hired for jobs and I don't. I feel like I am just as good at _____ as they are, but maybe I could work on:

AUDITION LOG

Casting Director:

Date:

Project:

Choreographer:

Callback: Yes / No

Wardrobe:

Self-Evaluation:

Feedback:

Notes:

AUDITION LOG

Casting Director:

Date:

Project:

Choreographer:

Callback: Yes / No

Wardrobe:

Self-Evaluation:

Feedback:

Notes:

AUDITION LOG

Casting Director:

Date:

Project:

Choreographer:

Callback: Yes / No

Wardrobe:

Self-Evaluation:

Feedback:

Notes:

You can download a version of this log at
www.MatthewShaffer.com

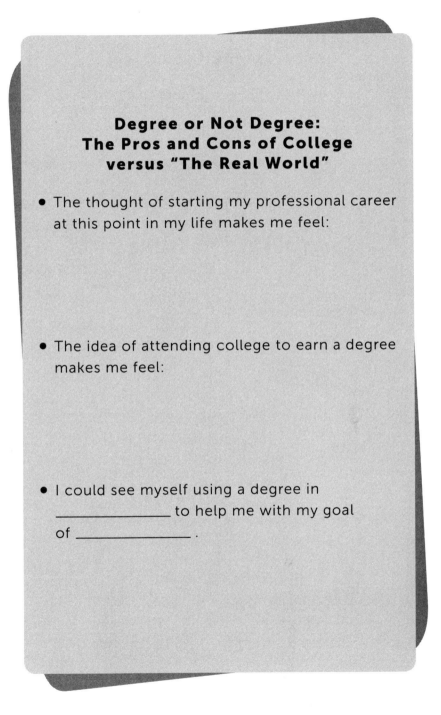

Degree or Not Degree: The Pros and Cons of College versus "The Real World"

- The thought of starting my professional career at this point in my life makes me feel:

- The idea of attending college to earn a degree makes me feel:

- I could see myself using a degree in _____ to help me with my goal of _____ .

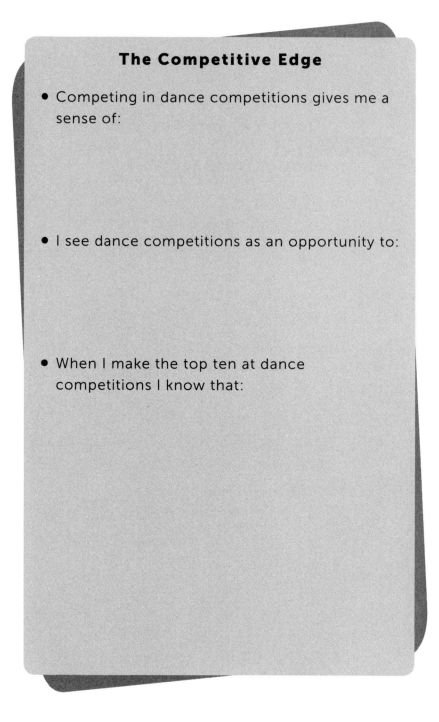

The Competitive Edge

- Competing in dance competitions gives me a sense of:

- I see dance competitions as an opportunity to:

- When I make the top ten at dance competitions I know that:

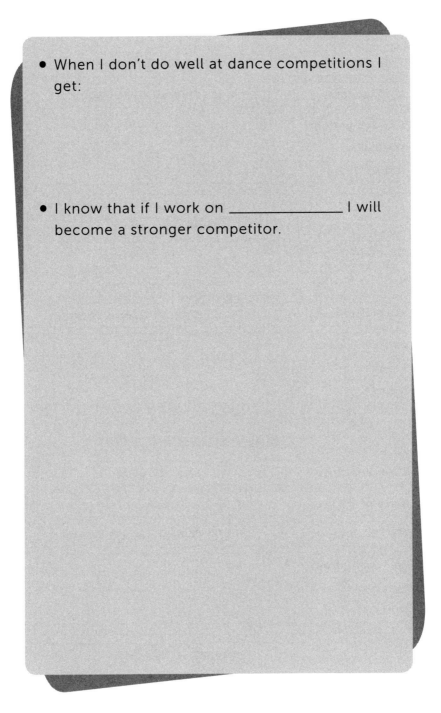

- When I don't do well at dance competitions I get:

- I know that if I work on _____ I will become a stronger competitor.

COMPETITION TRACKER

Competition:

Date:

Title of Dance:

Choreographer:

My Placement:

Overall Group Winner:

Self-Evaluation:

Feedback:

Notes:

COMPETITION TRACKER

Competition:

Date:

Title of Dance:

Choreographer:

My Placement:

Overall Group Winner:

Self-Evaluation:

Feedback:

Notes:

COMPETITION TRACKER

Competition:

Date:

Title of Dance:

Choreographer:

My Placement:

Overall Group Winner:

Self-Evaluation:

Feedback:

Notes:

TIP

You can download a version of this log at
www.MatthewShaffer.com

About the Author

MATTHEW SHAFFER is a true multihyphenate. He wrote, directed, and starred in his first production when he was seven years old and has been entertaining audiences (and family members) ever since! When Matthew isn't busy performing on stage and screen, he is traveling the globe as a choreographer, master teacher, and dance judge and continues to collaborate and create work with Jeff Payton and their production company, A Group Production, in Los Angeles. For more, please visit www.matthewshaffer.com and follow him on Instagram and Twitter @funnyshaffer.